The Plane of Bliss
On Earth As It Is In Heaven

R A M T H A

JZK Publishing
P.O. Box 1210
Yelm, Washington 98597
360.458.5201
800.347.0439
www.ramtha.com
greg@ramtha.com

The Plane of Bliss was edited by
Debbie Christie, Greg Simmons
and Pat Richker.
Brett Alt (cover design)

Other Titles by JZK Publishing:

The Mystery of Love (audio/book)
The Mystery of Love (CD/book)
A Beginner's Guide To Creating Reality

ISBN: 1-57873-026-0

Table of Contents

PREFACE

Greetings, my beloved people. That which you are about to hear or read is that which is a discussion upon topics familiar and unfamiliar, topics that are essentially the barest mystery of human wondering and human contemplation. It is about life in the continuum state, both preexistent and in incarnation. It addresses death and life and the burdensome and troublesome concepts of attitudes blocking the way of the master within. It redefines that which is termed self more akin to God than not. It is about the fracturing of self, the human divinity in support of attitudes that belong nowhere but are kept in the past, thereby keeping you in the past. You never get to fully enjoy nor engage the marvelous myth and legend of the possibility of the divine human, and I do mean you.

It is for you to understand that some of the techniques that will be addressed here are techniques that are only taught in this ancient school of wisdom. The techniques are disciplines that allow a shift in consciousness and altered states to bring about brain activity from the neocortex to the midbrain, high main brain stem, and in the lower cerebellum. These are different areas of consciousness and different spheres. These disciplines that are mentioned casually to the student body are not known to you; thereby do not endeavor to try them until you have properly learned that discipline.

When we are talking about energy moving to the brain, we are not talking about that which is termed an outside stimulus creating an energy rush. We're talking about an innate natural way in which energy intercourses the brain for the brain to bloom into one and in this to form properly the images of the perfect language of God. [1] Thereby any and all questions that you may have further about what you hear, you may inquire as to the source of this tape or transcript. [2]

I bid you good well. So be it.

---

[1] The perfect language of God is referred to as symbols or holograms formulated in the brain through imaging.

[2] Supplemental information and knowledge regarding what is discussed in this book can be found in all Beginning C&E audio tapes and also the book "A Beginner's Guide to Creating Reality."

I.
Introduction
Choosing the Spiritual Path

O my beloved God,
this night I am grateful
for my life
above all else.
Everything else
is illusion.
This life,
the blood
that pumps in my veins,
is you, my holy Spirit,
and everything else
is illusion.
Of this night
I do celebrate
that which I am
as God manifest.
My beloved father,
my beloved mother,
of these days
lift me from my turbulence
and set me upon
the ground of your being.
So be it.

To life.

We are going to talk about heaven. Heaven, the Plane of Bliss. We are going to start this teaching by you understanding an important aspect of yourself. You wanted the spiritual journey in this life. You wanted it. You're here because I dreamed this time for all of you, even those of you who are not here, those that are gathered in other places, a gathering place, a time of maturity, given eons to play out the human experience. But aside from that, you also had to be ready. Now this is important for every individual in this audience to understand because from that is a springboard to understand the rest of this teaching and to understand this school and your journey in this school. Every decision starts with you. And so the ultimate reason for being here is I provided that which is termed the hub and you came. But you had to be ready to come.

So what I want you to understand is that everyone in this audience chose in this lifetime to evolve themselves spiritually. Now that is important for you to understand because it empowers you to understand the meaning of this life and perhaps the journey of this life and that the true destiny of life, and particularly this one, is not about what you accomplish; it is about becoming. That is what is important in this life.

Now there is no one here that should ever say that they're here against their will because that is not the way that it is set up. Everyone is here freely in engaging in that which is termed the knowledge and its practices by choice.

There are entities who are here who are not here for the ultimate spiritual reason. They are here because people they are interested in are here. Now these individuals are gray individuals. And they don't really have that which is termed a specific destination in this life. Their destination is other people. And their destination is belonging to other people or finding importance in other people. There are those individuals that, because it is gray, the teachings and that which is termed the instruction and the disciplines, though practiced moment to moment and some moments ardently and other moments insincerely, are not consistent because they are not here really

7

by choice. They are here by choice of someone else.

Now that starts to eliminate and to weed some of the difficulties from this great family that you're in, understanding why people do certain things, why they're incapable of the spiritual order, to be able to perform some of the disciplines is because they don't belong here. And in reality they don't really know where they belong, only that they must belong to someone else.

Aside from those specific individuals, the majority of this group chose to be here in this lifetime. And hard as that may be for some of you to swallow, because when you're here and it's going well, you're happy for the journey, but when you leave this and you go out in the marketplace and you put back on your fleshy body, you find a conflict between the ongoing physical reality that you keep repeating and the spiritual reality that was really the destiny for being here. So there is a gap in destiny and in the follow-through of that destiny in the human incarnation. But that has always been apparent.

Given that then, I want each of you to understand that somewhere you made a choice then to be here and that you made a choice about this, about really dedicating a life, a human life, a human incarnation, to the sole development of the spiritual self, and that's why you're here. If this was not your destiny, you wouldn't be here tonight, or you wouldn't be in this school, or you would be the gray in-between entity who is not wholly here any time they're here. They're only here because of someone else.

Now if we can take in a state of human and spiritual maturity and grasp this as a truth, then the truth empowers us. When we do not grasp this and are still wondering why we are here, we are not empowered by what we learn. We first must be empowered by recognizing that there is a self who is divine that can be empowered. That's why it is important for an entity to recognize their actions as their actions, because it's always defining self and always empowering self.

Blame, as a side note, is a disingenuous quality of the spiritual person because blame then unempowers the self. When you blame someone else, you are draining the powerful resources of self. And so what happens to self is that self then starts to be hidden under that which is termed the fog of misunderstanding. Here in this school it is important that self always be the core, and that power must always be generated from that core and that that power from that core at no time should be ever given away to someone else. And blame and victimization, those aspects of human characteristics, are the most important ingredients in removing the place of power from self and giving it away.

In order to fulfill this journey here, self must be defined and it must be defined not only as the spiritual self, but the spiritual self must be definable within the human self. And all of this defining and polishing leads to the impeccable life, the empowered life.

Now if you chose then this life for this spiritual journey, then that empowers you because it gives the place of destiny to you and that's where it should belong. That then is also consistent with you as a God having free will, the will that is free enough to imagine the unimaginable, but the unimaginable springing from the core of self along with its power. If we abolish then the self, through blame and victimization and living in the past, we then unseat the very aspect of the spiritual journey. We *disenthrone* * the God inside of us in favor of past incidents that we can blame our miserable, wretched, and failing existence upon. That is an undefined self, a power utterly given away, that when such a creature endeavors to manifest, there is not the thrust from the core self in order to bring it forward. If no one is on the throne, the unimaginable cannot be imagined. Furthermore, there is no power to do it, to do anything with.

Well, when I then, from the first moment I appeared here, said you are God, that you were all God — forgotten, yes— it is my job to help you remember. That is the nucleus of the spiritual journey, and you chose to be a part of that journey, to define God, to define God and to seat that divinity within self. God, to define God, and when we do so, self becomes definable.

It is only when we have defined the self do we get to occupy it. It is only when we occupy it do we then become utterly empowered for the unimaginable. Up to that point, it is not going

---

* *Ramtha from time to time coins words to make a point or to emphasize his teachings. These words are in italics throughout these writings.*

to work; never will.

Now this destiny, before you came into this life — and we're going to talk about the place of Bliss — was an option seen that all of you except for a few were ready to take on. We're going to understand that in a deeper aspect.

But I want to at this particular point say to you that unless self can be empowered fully, then the spiritual life, that which you came here to experience, will never be realized. The walk of the master will never be walked by you until you leave no footprints in yesterday. Because the past was the generation of growth, that meant essentially the giving away of power to greater elements of authority. And that authority could have simply been your classmates in the first grade, at the beginning of what we call social consciousness, or giving your power away to your parents and the way that you were raised. That then starts the bleeding, if you will, of a life that is disjointed and that seemingly has no purpose but to coast and to ride and to barely get by. It is a life that the unimaginable is not a part of; it is only what is in trend and what is easy.

Now the spiritual walk of the master means — and for this we are going to have to manifest in your life what is called revelation, so that it is revealed to you on each of your individual levels what the past and my term for it really means. We can never abolish the memories of who we were, but what we must do is transmute the energy of what we were, a *disenthroned* entity searching for self, and we must take the energy that we have in the neuronet off of it and bring the power of that neuronet to continuously repeat day after day after day those circumstances of your past because it's up here — it's hard-wired; it's happening up here — that that hard wiring takes the power and distributes it, to hold in place that which the past dictated. That is unacceptable for a student in the spiritual work because, number one, there is no spiritual work without power and, number two, there is no power without a sense of self. And if self has not been reclaimed and redefined, then there is no such thing as the unimaginable, as man or woman being master of reality. It doesn't work; it hasn't worked.

10

So in understanding that, the past means to abolish victimization, to abolish envy, jealousy, hatred, malice, to abolish that which is termed the aspects that are so degrading to the spiritual self, that literally strip it of its beautiful power and hold together the demons of our own mind. The stripping of all of that means taking responsibility for those actions and making the responsibility one of self. And when we do, then the blaming no longer is locked up in your pitiful parents — who, by the way, are spiritual people as well — or locked up in your first-grade class. It's no longer locked up in your need to be needed.

When you say, "I created this. I cannot tell you why I created it or when I got the idea to create it, but I did it; otherwise it would never have occurred," you no longer have the outlet of continuous blame focused on entities or an entity in your life. Suddenly the cord is cut, the chains are cut, and the self begins to be defined.

Now this is a mournful moment because human beings by nature are cowards. They're cowards. And why are they cowards? Because they are afraid to be confronted by their own choices. And so in a state of fear we run and point a finger at someone else. And pointing the finger at someone else is our cowardly way of excusing the circumstance. When we do that, when we point this finger of power, then that means that this mind of power has focused the energy, reflected it back off of us to someone else and thus we are dethroned. It is not a simple measure, I assure you, to take responsibility for our life, but it is the bravest spiritual part that does, no matter how painful it may be. And do you know what pain is? The coming home of the prodigal son of energy.

We call this then the dark night of the soul. All of that suffering now is full bore upon us because it's energy returning to the source. But it is through the suffering that we are purified because once the energy passes the barrier of the emotional body and the emotional body is disturbed and ruffled and the heart beats fast and the breath is shortened and the tears begin to roll, that means that energy is coming back and it's passing through the barrier of the emotional body and it's causing a storm. And, you know, you have to live in the storm. It's the nature of the child coming home. And when the storm is over, energy, now being purified through the emotional body, has returned full cycle and its coming home is a necessary ingredient in defining the self, that which we are.

Now no one is ever going to make you take credit for your life. You can give lip service to this, but the true warrior is one who does it and does it very well — it's the conquest of self — and does it in a fashion knowing full well that what they've put out is coming back home manifold. It is the one who does this that in the end is liberated.

All beings who in Bliss chose the spiritual life, they know that in making such a choice, it is not the easy path, that it is a path of defining the self and polishing it, and they can't even imagine what that is going to mean in their life until they get into it. And do you know it is at this junction that most people turn tail and run? Why? Because — it's simple — unless the divine that we are sits within the throne of this temporal body, it can never create the marvelous unless it has divined and defined in ourselves. And unless that happens, the unimaginable is not going to happen to you, nor will that which is termed the righteous happen to you.

These measures of myth, dream, and legend always then remain that to the chronic victim. And as they remain that, we marvel at those who seem to get through and do the miraculous. We are marveling at one who has passed the bridge, who has made the journey, the journey into recalling power back to self and has lived through it. Those who cannot face it and are cowards and run from it are never again empowered with the lucidity, clarity, and the ability to move as a master because only until self is defined can a master then be born. It can never be born out of undifferentiated self.

You understand about the core defining self and its power? You understand that giving that power away depletes the core? Now you notice that when I refer to the past that I always refer to your greatest obstacles. And seemingly in reference to that which is termed the past, it seems as if I think that the past was all terrible. No, it was all purposeful.

Now what I want you to understand is that all the beautiful things in your life, all of those things that you did and were done to you that are sweet, those could only have occurred in a moment of self-definition, so they are always with us because they are the core of what we are. That is the reason why in religions that God is always pleading with His flock to be good and to do good deeds and to be men and women of moral and impeccable values because there is a truth in that. And the truth is that when we elect to be that way, we have not given any power away but have been empowered. And the more that that empowerment occurs, the more awesome the entity's reality; that's the way that it works. All of you are endeared with beautiful and sweet moments in your past. Those moments don't have to be thrown away because they are integral to the defining of self.

So now if those defining moments are the lofty moments in our life, they can be seen as acts of the simplest things that you did, from the moment of your cognitive memory of what was done to you, what you did to others, all through your life; those are empowered moments. That's the true self expressing.

But for the most part, you live in a dynamic society to which blame and cowardliness in favor of image is a way of life here. And it is the dog-eat-dog, the hyena preying upon the young. It is success motivated and feared, God almighty, by the aspects of failure. These then become the dynamic in which a past that is grievous, a past in which power has been given away, in which there is victimization and blame and the pointing of fingers, begins often now at a very early age. Then we see why that it is important to address the past in terms of energy and the terms of giving it away and staying confined in a mode of consciousness and its neuronet of being the eternal sufferer and the eternal victim.

No master is this. Nor will you find sympathy from any master at your election to being this. Why? Because every master knows that every life's action is a personal choice and that that personal choice is a free-willed choice, and that any master who is a master understands and knows that, without sympathy or empathy. Very clear distinctions here in what you're learning. And the distinction is that the master now has seated the self firmly in its divine room and now from this point navigates that divinity towards a life that is based entirely upon the crucial contemplative meditative placement of energy. That's the master.

So now having said that and reminding all of you that you are here by choice — you chose this life as a life to which the spiritual will become revealed to you — now we empower you utterly.

From this then we are going to back up and talk tonight about the Planes of Bliss; as some would call it, heaven.

Now over the years in your time we have discussed frequently that which is termed the interim existence, that interim existence being that which you were prior to this incarnation. And although I have not *languored* at great depth upon it, nor have I *languored* at great depth upon your past life, there is great and wonderful reason for that. For in my wisdom, I understand that those who do not have spiritual maturity cling to these in the same values as they have clung to their victimization, their tyranny, and their self-pity and it is giving more fodder to the animal within man and woman than it is that which is termed manna for the spiritual self. The focus here has been on becoming God. That is what is important and will always be important, but tonight we're going to talk about the interim place and the interim place to where all of you were before you were born.

Now I have stated boldly in the past that we do not create our parents; that is true. But also remember that we are drawn to a genetic pool that is only equal to what we are before arriving. So in that sense, subconsciously, we only become what we're capable of becoming. We can never become what we are incapable of becoming. In other words, we cannot be anything greater than what we are. So in the interim place we are talking about the third, fourth, and fifth levels. They are the planes of rest and restoration.

It becomes obvious then that the physical body has died and all of its energy, from the soul that gave it life, is pulling away from it. So the body goes into a slow state of decay. Without modern technology and the art of embalming, that which is termed the energy naturally would rapidly decay within a matter of a fortnight. And all decay is is the breaking down of coagulated matter and the release of the conscious pattern.

Here we are talking about the self. The self, the spiritual self, that which is not seen, has already departed up through infrared into the great tunnel of light to be met by the lords of light at the very end. And all of you went through the reading of your life. In elder times it was called judgment day. It is judgment day, except that it really isn't a judgment; it is to refresh your memory on what you did.

Understand that you are a being that is transpersonal but still personal. You are a being that is transmuted out of a fleshy body. You have gotten out of the garment. And here where there was such a delay in the Spirit working through the body to create reality — because you're living in a body that is mass to mass — now you're more in your own domain as a spiritual entity. You're actually vibrating in a kinder realm than this realm.

So there you watch your life. How is that possible? Because the bands that you are, that supported and gave and nourished life in the womb, take back with them as mind everything that you ever did because doing is an action and action is energy. And the focus of that energy is the patterns of mind. So we begin to watch the patterns of mind as they come together in a whole lifetime's effort.

Now let's pause here for a moment and let me tell you this: Every moment, every moment in the light of all eternity, will be weighed against a feather one day. Every moment counts. Everything that you do and I did is seen. And it is seen both as the observer and the participant, both as the doer and the done-to, everything. That is why it's called judgment day, because most ignorant people think, or they are under the delusion, that their thoughts aren't things. Their thoughts are things. And they are under the *delusionment* that what they do behind their closed doors no one knows but them. That is a delusion. Everything is known and everything will be shown. And in this heightened state it is necessary not for any one being to look at you and condemn you; it will be enough that we see it for ourselves. There is no harsher judge than the soul on judgment day.

Now when this occurs — and you're all at one point going to experience it because you've already experienced it — what is it that is meaningful from this? What is meaningful is how burdened are you by unfinished business? How burdened are you by unfinished experiences? If I tell you that you are God, then this life is to evolve that godhead as all. So how many experiences did you not own? And every time that you were cruel to someone, every time that you were cunning and undermining, every time that you bore false testimony against someone else, every time that you physically hurt someone, every time that your tongue lashed out in revenge and blame, every time that you meted out your fury of unrequited love to the destruction of those around you and yourself, every thing becomes you in that moment of viewing. You are everything, you know?

So then you suffer the attack of your *villainry* and you feel what it feels like. You become the child that you've beaten and you feel its helpless pain. You become that which is termed the abuser and the full onslaught of tempted intoxicating fury upon that which is innocent and cannot strike back. You feel what it is to be slandered upon and your good and gracious name abused and dishonored. You will feel that because you're God.

We are not separate in this hour. We are whole in this hour. We are driven to the understanding that more than any other time it is in this passing that we realize that we are the whole web of life. We feel the abandonment that we abandoned with. We feel the untruth that we are upon someone else. We feel the blame placed upon us unduly by us. We feel that which is termed the heartbreak of unrequited love, and we are the one who bore the chains of that blame. We are honored and dishonored. We are amused and bemused. We see how we prostituted our values.

We become the body in its agony and in its abuse. We become the abuser and the abused, and this is judgment. And we feel it full-width. We revel in the dream and in the inspiration that we had at five, and we despair in the losing of that dream at twenty-three. We become the dream and then we fade as the dream. We become the inspiration that we marveled at and then we become the boredom of inaction. We see the instigation of new ideas and concepts that we came up with and we are then the idea itself, the thought form, and we see it as an unnurtured and unloved egg that never hatches. And we see the idea that never came into fruition and the pain of its *uninclusiveness* into our environment. We see it all because we are all God.

The subjective element in all of this is very important because the core of self is subjective because it is everything, so the self becomes more enriched and more defined in this view.

We see how many times we needed to beg someone's pardon, and we see all the times we didn't ask it of ourselves. We see all the times that we could have loved but, in our selfish renegade self, minted none out, and we see the vacuous place to where love lives not and we are driven in emptiness and despair. We see it all.

And in this exposé we find wholeness even in the suffering, that rarefied moment. And how do I describe suffering without a body? Well, emotion, though it is generated by electrical stimuli from the brain from neuronets and then dominoed in the body through the release of hormones, it becomes a living thing. It is an energy field. And it is with that energy field that we stand and we are then immersed within all of this energy. We cannot undo it. It is done. The die has been cast.

Now this is not a bad thing, but it's a necessary thing for the ignorant, and you all are. Because what we do with such a vision is that we then become encumbered. We become encumbered by the difficulties in which we see. An encumbrance is a wonderful term because what it really says is all of these things that we did, we did to ourself. And it is through this revelation that we must unencumber and give to the self love, which God is. God is giving; remember?

So then we walk away from this in deep *ponderance*. We are given any sort of image we wish to ponder this in. Some ponder on high mountain ranges in Bliss. Some ponder behind great and noble trees. Some ponder by beautiful lakes surrounded by dappled woods. Some ponder in great libraries. Some ponder floating in the midst of nothing because it can't tolerate anything to be around them. But *ponderance*, the art of contemplation, always follows this. And what becomes inescapable is that we have done this to ourself because we are all the self.

Now here is the stickler. The stickler is that these acts, this life, grew out of a very slow time, that the whole focal point of this life was the human body. So no matter what you do on the Plane of Bliss, you can never reconcile there what you did on the plane of flesh. We cannot manifest on the Plane of Bliss the experiences that will bring about physical emotion because we are without them.

Oh, we contemplate and then imagine, like I did by the fire in dreaming this journey. We imagine and, as soon as we imagine, all of the forms and the scenes appear; instantly they appear. And as we contemplate we watch ourselves and how we deal with what we dealt out. And we imagine. And because we are in the Plane of Bliss to where there is no mass to mass, our self is more akin to that time, which is no time, as it is referred to here. So there, the moment that we imagine something, it appears exactly as we imagine it. And so our surroundings are always changing.

And in contemplation this is ideal because when we contemplate, we can visually see the exact scene and how we would like it to happen. And try as we may, however, to get relief from that, we cannot get relief from it. What it does provide us with is our divinity. And our gift to image has allowed us to reconstruct the past, to reconstruct the past and to move from that point forward. However, this mapping, though thoroughly researched, could take thousands of years on Bliss. Contemplation on Bliss is much different than contemplation here.

And we may *languor* there and plot and plan and we may seek it out in these planes. The moment the idea occurs to us that there are great beings with this wisdom, they appear. And they appear and teach us. And they help with our model of imagination. They do not change the model in the time of contemplation. The thoughts are given to you and you incorporate the wisdom into the picture. That's how it works, because it's not their picture; it's your picture.

K nowledge. If knowledge to you means then a reservoir of information flowing through a computer, a computer will appear and will have dendrites connected to you, and then the knowledge will flow through the computer. But ultimately the knowledge flowing back to you, you must be the program that incorporates it.

Or you may envision knowledge in great halls of learning, in the great halls of academia. And you may envision this knowledge in a set of rare books, and so immediately a great library will appear and you will not be able to see the end of it, and yet all of the great texts appear on old and ancient shelves. And in your mind old may mean that they are faded and they are covered in dust, and so they will be. And so you look for the dustiest, faded-est, cobweb-covered manual you can find, because in your mind that's the one that will have all knowledge, and you'll find it. And you have a table. You can sit down, you can have an electric lamp, you can have a candle, you can have an oil lamp, you can have a florescent lamp, and you sit down and you read. You read, by the way, every page, a page that looks like soft light and letters that are multidimensional, and they jump off the page into you and you think you're reading. And it's the same knowledge.

And what you walk away from, in spending a hundred years in this library, is information on how to modulate the room of contemplation, the room of how you are going to make it different, to elongate this burden, the *enburdenment* that you have of being unfinished, of the error as you see it that you have done to another. How would you be able to justify that? And how would you be able to write it? You'll figure it all out.

Now it is not by accident that this is starting to act exactly like a quantum field of potential. Well, it is. The Plane of Bliss is at the quantum level, so when an entity — that is spiritual without the body— is rarefied mind, the moment occurs immediately.

So what is the entity doing? The entity is selecting paths of intentional destiny, creating them in a linear fashion with or without the help and endeavoring to find a resolve, because no one wants to live being all things punished and punishable. That realm is called hell. But one lives in it as unresolved and burdened, unfinished business.

Now remember, keep in mind, there is no one on this plane that will ever tell you you are right and wrong. You're the ones that do that; there is no right and wrong. But it becomes immensely clear to us that we are of the angelic realm and that we really are foreign travelers in an alien world and that we really are empowered to recreate that world according to our imagination, our greatest resource. And so no one there is to say this is right and wrong. I tell you the more God you are in that moment of light review, you will feel the blow of everything measured out by you in incarnation, because how could God be anything else but everything?

Now the hall of contemplation. Very important. There are beings that are still there that have been mapping a potential lifetime very carefully. They've been there for hundreds of thousands of years. They're mapping it. And they're sort of like the watcher-at-the-gate story I told you about, watched everyone come in. Well, there are entities that post themselves at heaven's great gate and watch everyone coming in with all their stuff, and they learn. But what is important is it's not meaningful learning until it is applied on the level in which the wisdom was generated.

Now I am telling you about the plane in ordinary tongue that is much more illustrious, much more dynamic, much more fantastic, and much more beautiful than this common speech can allow. I am endeavoring to bring it home to you, a very valuable lesson which we're going to learn about, the remarkable self and to understand why you chose to be here.

Now an encumbered entity. An encumbered entity who has got a lot of unfinished business here, unless they have a physical body working in this time, they cannot finish it. They can dream it on those other levels, but those dreams will never be able to be experienced until they are borne in the time to which they were meant.

Now an encumbered entity then has drawn out the linear path, has gotten as much help as they know to ask. And when they are ready to return, they are drawn into genetic pools that are equal to where they left off.

In this Plane of Bliss — in heaven, as some would have it to be called; the greater planes I call them — there is no regret at being there. I want you to know never was a place more lively and more beautiful than this place because it's the unimaginable imagined. And never was there such a state of being that utterly was free of the encumbrances of slow time and slow matter. And never was there a place to where physical beauty wasn't the most important thing, because there you could take on any appearance that you wanted, so it wasn't important. Here it's important; there it's not important because it's changeable. So then everyone is free from that, so you are floating closer to God. You are in a state shadowed by the golden realm. You're in a state to where it can be the eternal day or the eternal night. And there are multitudes there and it seems as if there is room for everyone. Well, there is. Now it's a deserving place to be. It is the place of rest before the next battle.

So it's not like some of you who are sort of prone to suffering anyway to see it as a place to where you *languor* in the contemplative forests and suffer. No, but that is important as the subjective aspect of God to be able to feel what you did. But you're always objective. And from that, there is no grief about leaving your family. There is no grief about leaving your husbandmen, your wives, your friends, your neighbors; you don't have that sort of emotion because you're free of all of that.

And there is a knowingness that permeates these realms that what is happening on the earth plane is a great big drama. And you played a part. What is important is that you never finished your lines. And that coming out of that thick dream, you know your children were not left behind; they always will be. And coming out of that, you didn't leave behind your love; your love is with you, always will be. Because when we become the subjective God, we interface with all life, so how could we be separate from it? It is in such a state that it is difficult to understand, but you've all been there. You have all been there; otherwise you couldn't be here now.

Now stop grieving for a moment and suffering and understand that in this encumbered state is what generates us to our greater power. And we want to design a life and lay it out and imagine it and change the patterns, the players; anyone that wants to volunteer can move into it. We want to do that before we return and pick up where we left off. Now that's very important.

Now I want to back up and talk about the players involved in the upcoming drama. What has always been considered, that people who meet and have a kinship for one another met in a past life, that's not so. Try this one on: How about that you never met before and met on the Plane of Bliss because you had both come to the same encumbrance, that you both arrived at the same forest to contemplate the same thing. Some of these places are very crowded. And we always gravitate to what we are.

And so, you see, the players that will play an integral part in the upcoming life don't have to be anyone that we were before. And to always delude yourself into thinking, that shows the sign of your ignorance about the spiritual life because this place isn't everything and these lifetimes aren't everything. We will have beings that will meet in the same place of contemplation that, my God, may be extraordinarily advanced entities whose past incarnations were geniuses or great leaders and, you know, they have a flaw and that flaw brought them in contact with you. Or they may be coming from another terrestrial planet in which that flaw they can work out on this one. We meet through association of encumbrances.

Now those dynamics of such a meeting — and how difficult is this to understand — that when you sit by someone and you enjoin them in a conversation, you're bonding with them. And pretty soon you are moving through the labyrinth of their mind, understanding what they're saying to you; you're into them. And they in turn are moving through the labyrinth of your mind. That's what we call conversation. If you understand that, then you can begin to grasp the concept that association of encumbrances brings like to like when shared upon in that rarefied place. It is not about talking. You don't talk. Your thoughts proclaim. And so each of you engage in each other's thoughts.

It's at those times that in engaging in each other's thoughts we find a marvelous and wonderful thing happens called mercy. In this wonderful kingdom then, this life that we've laid out for ourself, we have found someone who has the same encumbrance, but the encumbrance may be that that entity had done to them what we did. And though we are both done-to and did in this place of contemplation, our minds come together and formulate a relationship, and those relationships then form a later meeting on this plane.

So it's not about who you knew two thousand years ago or four thousand years ago. The most meaningful ones are the ones that you meet in Bliss because they've arrived at the same place. Now these people will come in and out of your life, often to fulfill the very drama that you came back here to play out. And which role are they playing now? It's ultimately selective at that moment. When they viewed their life and they did an unthinkable to someone else, they can *restrategize* that to where the unthinkable then is done to them. And the player that will be involved is one who was the victim in the earlier existence. They're learning balance. And yet they only may appear and then disappear out of our life, but that's what we're here for.

There is no such thing as chance. Everything is created from consciousness, and consciousness does not simply hold itself as sole purpose on this plane; it is all planes. And the closer we are to Point Zero, the more pure we are as conscious beings. So this great and wonderful realm, that the moment you think it is, is our true nature, entities. That is our true nature; that is what we're used to. What we are not used to is being logged down and burdened down by slow time and the mechanics of the physical body because there we are liberated from it, from all that it represents.

So now when we set out in our memorable engagement with

other beings there, when we set this pattern out and we have decided upon this potential line, then we are ready to return. Those that we have blended with before, we will meet again. We won't remember them but we will meet them, and the soul will know because the Spirit recalls the conversation. The soul recalls the journey. It's just the corporal mind, the corporal brain of the physical entity that is yet to be born that will not remember this incident.

So when we are ready, we come back because we can go no further unless we come back here and take care of this unfinished business, until we understand completely that God is one. And that when we are one, when we decide to be one, is when we have selected the spiritual journey, a life filled with that.

Now understand also that there are entities on these planes that although they too are burdened down by encumbrances, their greatest encumbrance is the lack of success because they never got to be that, so they're naturally going to formulate lines of potential to which they are born. They are born in the backwater and they have to move through this life and become a success from out of shambles. That's the way their drama will be played out. It's very important for them. And someone must be the fall guy in the play. And you know why they must be the fall guy? Because those are the entities who stepped on other people to attain success in their previous lifetime. And so the meaningful minds come together for this wonderful display.

So there are people whose encumbrances are the lack of success, for example, and they are going to then lay down that potential of a whole life, a large sandbox to which they play the game for that one fleeting moment of glory, and that's all the life would have been worth was that fleeting moment. And then it becomes degenerated because it will reflect only on that one moment and it will become its past.

The plethora of why's are multiple. Unrequited love works the same way. And in these incidents, it usually has to do with that which is termed love. If love has been unfulfilled in another situation or another lifetime, love is given, yet not received or rejected. More often that character will not be in the place of contemplation the same time you are. But who will be there will be those who suffered the same thing. And they then set up their life to emerge and to find one another and to find love fulfilled. It's important because God is love. They will set it up as the learning of the neophyte in the processes in the material world. There are entities who never completed because their encumbrances before coming into that life to where they met were burdensome and toilsome and demanded much of them; yet when they meet, they are like two souls in one. Their lives may have been cut short or been pledged to others and there the longing is so strong. The most powerful tie there is in Bliss is love; that if they were fortunate enough, one will wait for the other in the room of contemplation. And they'll always meet them there because if love is that deep then it is God self-on-self, the reward of a lifetime. And that entity will wait and will meet that entity in the room, who that entity will find because they are as one. In their union they understood that God is, because between the two of them they were one and that one became the seed that would cause a *flourishment* in the rest of their life. Now they wait for one another, rejoice in one another, and they love one another. And do they have bodies to love? Absolutely. Do they have bodies to make love? They will make them. Everything is imaginable; everything is allowed.

And what do they want? They can have anything that they want and they revel in each other's presence because there is no lack in love, none. If there is, then it is yet to be matured. It is not the mature level of love to which I am speaking. No lack.

Now these two entities, because of their impassioned love, if they were yet unable to live it out and wish a desire to, then they plot a plan to which they address their encumbrances individually; and then when their encumbrances have been met and fulfilled, they meet. It's like the reward. But they don't know that, once they're born. They only feel a pull, a drawing, a recognition.

And there are enemies that meet; there are enemies that meet.

Hatred is the same thing as love; it's as intense. And old enemies meet in the fields of contemplation. I met many of them. What do enemies do? Well, they are not enemies. They are not enemies. In the field of contemplation they join a reunion. And in that reunion they then can patch it up on the physical plane, owning it once and for all by reengaging the opportunity in the twentieth century. And perhaps what were once enemies of a dreadful battle at sea, and one succumbed and the other victorious, perhaps in the twenty-first century they will be corporate enemies.

Now that you understand encumbrances a little bit better, you begin to see then that those entities that we have met in this lifetime were not met by accident, that each person that we met along the way was actually part of a line potential that we created in Bliss.

And what is interesting about the mapping in Bliss is that it very rarely ever acts out on earth like it did in Bliss. We have a tendency to paint things very cheery in Bliss. We forgot what it felt like to have a blister on our hands from gripping too tight. We forgot what it was like holding too tight. We don't know that. That's why that in the material realm, when all of this falls into place, it's a remarkable adventure because its maturation is much different than how we planned it before and then we held the element of the bare mystery of enchanted forgetfulness. That also plays into it and is supposed to play into it.

So all lives that come together in this life aren't necessarily recognized from before, and you shouldn't try to do that because in trying to do that, sometimes you may muddy the picture of the potential that you're endeavoring to find here. We're endeavoring to find self. We are endeavoring to do it with clarity and purity, without any pollution whatsoever, the rawest of our beautiful nature. And the more that we can demystify it, the more real it will become.

When we, in order to reconcile every situation, try to frame it in cosmic text, we oftentimes muddy the picture. Relationships don't have to be cosmic — that's a joke — they only need to be relationships. And from that raw and dynamic center we are going to come closer to the plan than if we tried to take it out of context and make it into something it never was, because then we find the encumbrances of creating phantoms that only begin to bother us.

So in reality oftentimes every life that fulfills the contemplation room that we create — however long, however complicated, however short — our true and wonderful friends are really the emergence from the future, never the past, because in the Plane of Bliss is where the future is born.

So then most individuals here start out with good intentions, and their plan never comes into real fruition because they get stuck. Now this is an important message about the past. When you get stuck in the past, you deny yourself your future potential. And that's what is so grievous about your acts of holding onto your victimization, your suffering, your anguish, your parents did this, they did that. Why sacrifice what was created in Bliss for holding onto that which is temporal in the flesh?

When we give our power away to enslaving factors of yesterday, we diffuse the self to which the potential in Bliss we created it for and from. And when we no longer have self, because we have *disempowered* it through grief and suffering and misery and anxiety and all of that, we stop the flow of our true destiny. And all we get is the garbage that we cling to for the sake of self-identity.

And why not? It's served you well so far. It's enslaved lovers, it's made people to feel sorry for you, you've used it to get your way, you've used it against other people, you've used it upon yourself. It's served you. Why would you want to get rid of it? Because unless you do, you don't get the great future that you have created for yourself and all the marvelous beings that joined you in its creation and you with them, who will touch your lives in unimaginable ways, who will move your soul in waves of fire you have never known, who will inspire you towards your ingenious self, of which no one hereto of your past has been able to do. You designed a destiny to unencumber yourself and, in that, the great minds participated in the making. When we then release to that, we get out of the way and let it come. Our clinging nature to yesterday only is going to take us back through this process and we're going to still be encumbered by what we have not met. And for a very materialistic term, we're going to be the lesser for the greatness we denied ourself made in heaven. Past-life relationships can also be further developed in that which is termed the contemplation area or period. Entities who arrive there, having shared the same experiences though incomplete, will often find themselves in the same room; as an example, an unresolved conflict or unresolved issues that were left hanging when one perished and one stayed. The one perished has gone through the aforementioned process that I have taught you and is in the process, after rest, of finding themselves in the contemplation area. And, of course, what is one of the first things to come up is that they are burdened with this difficulty. And what makes it more agonizing, if you will, is that the issue was directly with another Spirit incarnate who was still on the terrestrial plane. So working it out, working around the issue, when we have some who stay and some who have gone, never putting to rest the experience, we have that entity or those entities who will work in the contemplation room around this burden, endeavoring to find ways to address it. And, of course, all imagination always works here instantly, so you imagined all sorts of things. But what always becomes baseline important is that it has to do with this entity representing self because there is power that has been placed there that has been disturbed in this experience that has not been culminated.

Now one of two things usually happens here. If the entity going through the contemplation where years are here, there are thousands of years there, or there is no time at all — everything works that way in the Plane of Bliss, so they may have fatigue and have worked out the entire plan of what they want, circumventing this experience, leaving it out of the next life plan, not facing it — then they will come back and go through that lifetime without facing this entity. And even if the entity who the issue is unresolved with then passes and goes to the same area of contemplation, it's going to find the same problem because now the roles are reversed. They are in and on the Plane of Bliss and their partner in the experience has now returned to the terrestrial life not even remembering who they are.

So then one has borne a new life without ever addressing this encumbrance in that next lifetime. There is an incompleteness about them, a shadow area. And the one who is now contemplating suddenly finds that to their amazement there is an early arrival on the Plane of Bliss and it's you-know-who. And you-know-who reviews their life and then goes to the contemplation room and runs into you-know-who's been waiting there. So eventually they get it worked out. So that's one way to bypass it and come back, which everything is your will.

Or the other way is to wait until both meet and then work it out. Because no matter what we do with other entities, we can apply the same meaningful change and potential that we're going to use this on everyone, but the true test will come when we meet the one that it's unfinished with.

So here's an idea, an example, if you will. It's easy to tell people that you're sorry. It's easy to tell people that it's okay, in your terminology. But then there will be one person that it isn't easy to say that to. So what has come really easy to you and quips to you then becomes very difficult. It's a key that that is an entity who you are working an encumbrance out here with. So there are lifetimes that find themselves coming together to work out in this particular plane.

But for the most part those who are truly evolving are always going to be meeting new and various beings that necessarily have never shared any incarnation together but share a general path leading to some point, some convergence, to where each find a common place in which to communicate with and then subsequently share that experience. Well, these are future experiences that have already been agreed upon. Families will find themselves strong-bonded families. But for the most part, families that have generally worked out all of their differences — their issues of taking their power away, have found love within one another, and have allowed — rarely ever meet again because everyone is working out what it is they have not finished so they can entertain the unimaginable that they got to imagine.

In other words, so many lifetimes are just repetitious and

repetitious and repetitious, repeating the same cyclical movements that are born in the soul, the same experiences that the cowardliness of the human element backs away from and does not allow the pristine movement of the soul to finish, take its power back and then make room for a marvelous destiny.

Now why do we do this? That why is a very broad understanding that takes lifetimes to understand, but I taught it to you in your first C&E. [3] You're explorers from Point Zero. You are making known the unknown. What is important to us is to imagine the dream and to bring it into fruition, give birth to it in an impossible, arduous and difficult realm. The dream must exist on all seven levels in order to be fully realized by the dreamer. When we're down here casting dreams in thick time, we're down here casting dreams in a thick time that we're not used to. We are creatures of an eternal imagination because that is how we are. We are consciousness and energy. We are builders of archetypes of thought. And from that then energy behaves to form those thoughts; it becomes the movement of them, if you will.

We are not creatures of the flesh. We never have been. But when we allow our flesh to give us away, to give us away and to fracture our divinity into personalities that hold old fires, old flames, old bitternesses, unresolved and unyielding, we are fractured. We are the self called God. And when we allow our bodies to fracture us, our power then is split as brother against brother. We are in war to our very nature. We are no longer whole and pristine. We're here to make known the unimaginable, not to rehash what is already known and to warp its sense of maturity into a state that *degradates* even us.

On this Plane of Bliss we get to carry with us our most recent likeness. And oftentimes it is very helpful, because like the great scar in my front and my back helped to remind me always of my own inflicted treachery. We get to keep our bodies in their most recent form to remind us of what we must unencumber. Do you understand? Or we can simply choose to be nebulous in form. However we want to present ourself, we may present ourself in that fashion. But while we're on the Plane of Bliss we

---

[3] C&E is the abbreviation for Consciousness and Energy, the discipline used to move energy in the body.

are in a state of bliss. We are in a state of communion with the highest levels of life and we're ever so close to the fountainhead of it all, the eternal Point Zero, as it's been come to be known, the whole unifying with the Void itself. Well, we are enjoying each other's company. We are enjoying the bliss, the harmony, the magic of a mind. We are that mind; we are that most divine revelation of imagination. As it stands before us, it twists and turns and changes at our every thought. That's what we really are, people, and always have been.

Why then would you say, "Why? To come down here just to live a couple of years so that we could work out something? I mean is it really worth it?" Well, of course it's worth it. When you know you're eternal, playing the part even for a year, it's worth it. What isn't worth it?

Our point here is that we're sort of the little Gods that tried but got caught. You know, we got caught and, in what I've been endeavoring to teach you about ever since you've been with me, we got caught in a garment whose whole nature is so utterly backward from our very own, who has to exist in this slow-moving, slow-time compelling existence that has alienated us from what our whole actually is.

We have to finish our business, not so that we can go home; we have to finish our encumbrances so that we can be free of this entanglement of our cowardly nature of human flesh, that we can finish it up, that the nature of the human has not been able to do.

I want to tell you something. When it is said that man is an animal, that is correct. Man is an animal because of his animal nature, the nature of strong survival, strong reproductive, and highly territorial. Some are solitary. Predators are cunning and strike from behind. They're not brave. The weak gather together in greater numbers to protect their boundaries, hoping that someone else will fall, but not them. This is the animal nature.

Now how close are you to that nature? I can tell you how close you are. The spiritual nature isn't even working when you launch an attack upon the innocent, when you flail your debtors with a cat-o'-nine-tails because they owe you, when you hate because you give, and you're territorial because you want to protect your boundaries, and you would jump at the chance to copulate. That's the animal. The body does that very well because that is the nature of the kingdom that it's derived from.

And brave men and women who are acting in a role of greatness never attack from behind. Only a coward and a predator, who are both the same, do that. If that's the way that this is, and who can deny it — and how far are you really from it other than that you have good table manners and you wear garments and you defecate in toilets and not on the plains — you're not that far removed from your animal nature. The first three seals are the animal nature. When that human has its way, it will always act like an animal because it's a coward. And I tell you it's the spiritual self — what I'm telling you that you really are — that is the only viable aspect of this incarnation that can truly address encumbrances and is equipped to handle them. The human is not. You know, you are a coward who lived in a tarnished past of suffering; that's your cowardliness. You're an animal.

If you have not been relieved from it or been strong enough to relieve yourself of it, then you have yet to be a spiritual person because the Spirit is what is best equipped to do this because it's after it. The Spirit is after the encumbrances because, first, it has to take its power back to regain its wholeness of self and, when it does, it's the one that says, "No more. This is finished. I created it. I am responsible for it. I forgive you. You're free." That is a spiritual person, isn't it? So what does the animal do? "You owe me." Doesn't it? It does. "And now that you're vulnerable, I'm going to get you." That's the animal.

So being an *altered* ego is not going to help you. Just because you're born down here, your genetics are not in your favor because they came from genetics that were trying to do the same thing. And remember you're only drawing the physical body that was closest to what you were. This is a continuing story.

Now we come back here not because anybody sent us back here; we sent ourselves. We're back here not to change the world but to change ourselves. We are back here to be realized, not *reforgotten*. We've come back here to finish this business up.

So now I want to ask you then in the light of what I've taught you about the Plane of Bliss, it becomes monumental, does it not, that these little heart tremors of the personality carry more weight than you could possibly know? It's not the success we accomplish on this plane that is remembered in the halls of Bliss. It is not about how much money you make. It is not about how much you don't make. It is not about how famous you were here or how infamous you were here. It is not about what you look like here. It is not about any of that that here is so important. There is, what did we do? That's what's important.

And it's important enough to bring Gods to human knees because our agenda is different than the human animal. Our agenda is to be unencumbered and then bring in the unimaginable. That's what this is about. That is what this is about. Have people before you done that? Indeed there have been. There have been people who have cleaned up their experiences, finalized them, and were free of them. And who were they? The brilliant people that are now scattered and peppered throughout history that were geniuses because they brought the unimaginable through. You know why? They had the power to do it because self was put back on the throne. It was gathered back together, pieced together, and put on the throne.

Very few of these individuals that are heroic in your history got there by bliss. Most of them paid dearly for their genius. In other words, they suffered, endured, proclaimed, and accomplished. In other words, they took the tiger on, didn't they? And that turbulent life led to the one thing they wanted to accomplish here, the unimaginable, that they already knew before they were incarnated here. They got above the human drama and became Gods once again. And if only for a moment, their star shined. That's all it took. It was over with then. It's finished.

Which brings me back to my introduction. You made the choice to be here and to choose spiritual learning in this life. I set the foundation and you came. Now there is one great union that all of us in this room, save for a few, have in common. We shared collectively a lifetime together, a very tumultuous, arduous, awe-inspiring great life. And you witnessed marvelous things: the ending of an old earth and the beginning of a new one. You witnessed the dying of the Gods and the birth of men and you marched the long march. That's what we share in common tonight. And for that love, borne throughout the pages of this march, resides this moment, which allowed this moment to have a place in the Void in the mind of God, that when you were ready to choose to know more, there was a place to come. And it is inevitable.

So why on the Plane of Bliss, in heaven, would you choose what you already are on the Plane of Bliss to realize down here if you know it up there? Good question? Yes, it is. Because what is realized up there, in order to be fully known, must be realized into the bowels of God and it has to be made known here because this is the cauldron; this is the alchemist's crucible here. The shining star dancing on midnight blue liquid suddenly recoagulates and comes down to that little ball of nickel in the bottom of the bowl again. So here we are. You have to do it here.

On the Plane of Bliss most all of you in here came through your labyrinth and your encumbrances — you still have encumbrances — but all of you had a place of love in you, a place to vacillate to. And you had something startling happen to you: You saw me leave the plane without dying. You never forgot that. Where did I go and how did I escape the decay and the rottenness of the body? How was I able to do that? You see, you got to see that. That's why the legend of Christ and the resurrection is so strong in Christian minds today. It's poignant because it is a longing. It is an unimaginable imaginable that has set its seed in the mind of many people. You will find this in all religious doctrine.

With me and my people, before all of that gibberish, I left and you saw it and that was it. In my true style, make a point and get on. Which makes you ask, "Where did he go? He's not on the Plane of Bliss. Where is he?" Well, I am on the Plane of Bliss. When you came back, before you got back, you remembered me and where I went. And love is unforgettable. It is so sweet. It is unforgettable because it lacks nothing. So in your labyrinth you asked the ultimate question, "What is the unimaginable for me?"

Now there's another group across the river asking the same question. That's the group that invented computers. Because that group is just now discovering that if they can create an idea on the *superplane* of existence and move it right along into the time line, that if they get it in this body they're about to be born into, and if they actually get it and it actually works, whether you know it or not those technological geniuses are starting to wake up to what you're already getting to know. In other words, they're behind you. They look like they're in front of you, but they're actually behind you because they're just learning to create. They're just learning; you already know that.

So this group then says, "What do I need to know? What do I need to unencumber myself with?" Well, you're asking a heap. But, after all, all you're asking for is unfinished business. And when it's done, what do you want? "I want to go where no man has gone before. I want to know. I want to go where the Gods dwell. I want to know what it is to be a master." And when you imagined what a master was, you thought of me. When you thought of the dell of the Gods, you thought of me and created in your mind where you thought I went. And this fascinating journey, this fascinating puzzle, this exercise, this toy labyrinth that you built in your potential imagination, got you strung out on being spiritual. Because, you see, you don't get it unless you ask for it. And somewhere along the way there must be an ideal come into human consciousness that trips it.

All through your history you have had wonderful beings that have come in and have circumvented the system, that have been so bold, so arrogant, so pure, as to stand ten feet above mediocre man. What made them so different? Because they were filled with the power of the holy Spirit instead of the power of the animal.

That's what made them different. Why did they come back? They came back to *reremind* you to "Never forget me. I'm going to make such an impression on you, you're never going to forget me because one day you're going to want to know what I am."

I'm an ideal. It has been necessary to sprinkle ideals historically for all civilizations to keep them from collapsing: some astonishing thing that happened at noon, an appearance or reappearance of phenomenon — you're beginning to understand where that comes from now — something to snap us from this dream, heavy melatonin dream, of the carnal life that wakes us up and then we click on up here. When we click on, we click on as spiritual beings and click off as human beings. I was your catalyst.

So now in the light of all eternity, why would you want to spend this lifetime developing your spiritual self? First you have to overcome your encumbrances, own the past, because it says to you, those of you who make it, that you really have come to understand that you've already done everything in human consciousness. My God, who haven't you been? My God, what haven't you had? My God, who haven't you hated and how many haven't you loved? How many times do you have to die? How many times do you have to get sick? How many times do you need to be successful to realize you never were a failure? How many times does it take?

You know, only an entity coming back here would know that "The only reason that I'm coming back here is that I must finish my business. But my unimaginable dream is to be a *superbeing.*" What greater dream is there than being God? There is none.

So you included this in your potential line and remembered me from an incident I did with you. That's what brought this into being and you chose it. You want to understand what has not been you. And you want to find deliverance from your burden and wholeness. And that wholeness speaks to a wholeness of the self, that once it is completely contained it will be ready for the emergence of the future that was created on the Plane of Bliss.

Everyone has character flaws; everyone here does. But what

is that? To what scale of perfection do we find flaws? No one here is perfect. There is no such thing as the perfect human. No matter how damn hard you try, you'll never get there because in order to be that, you're going to have to be as base as any animal and you're already too far gone the other way.

You came here through a line that you created on the Plane of Bliss to learn not what was already here but what could be here. And you came here to have something to bring up and to remind you of the experiences that you need to complete. And they can be completed as simply as you wish or as arduously as you wish, and then from that be utterly and totally free to incorporate what you've already created, an unimaginable beauty. I promise you no one ever goes backwards when they are free of their encumbrances. They are truly liberated. They're liberated from their animal. They are liberated from their suffering. They become whole. They find the self, that which they really are.

I told you three times this evening that our natural way of creating is instantaneously. You begin to understand why a God would become so fractured in a human, because what we get immediately has to be processed into coagulation for the human. And the human, who is always protecting boundaries, always checking out victims, always looking for survival and always needing the copulation, these are impatient qualities. Nature is the survival of the fittest. And when it comes to the animal, the animal must fit as the fittest in all these categories.

When we truly become human beings, we really fracture the holy in ourself because the impatient human cannot hold onto an unimaginable imaginable if that dream does not directly relate to its security, its sovereignty, its longevity, its basis of copulation, and its superiority amongst unequals. The human will never hold a dream that does not facilitate its animal nature. That is the reason why the human is impatient and always riddled with doubt when it comes to imagination.

And here we are, the very Gods that made this creature

instantaneously. We revel in the imagination as true reality but cannot enjoy it to the root of God on this plane because the body that we inhabit cannot hold onto it and rejects it, thereby denying us access to that experience.

The body is not a dreamer. It can create thoughts. It is the computer. It can hold them *holographically*. But it finds it tiring to hold onto them. The God is the moment. It is the dreamer. And it needs to be strong enough in the body to be able to bring the dream forth instead of emasculate it.

This is a battle because always what happens is the body wins and the Spirit loses. And so there we go into a fall, into another meaningless life, that the only thing we're going to do when we die is go back and see the same program over and have to go and readdress in the same contemplation. Oh, we will be happy and relieved. But there is a greater calling for us, even there.

We are unfinished here. The spiritual journey and the walk of the master start when very painful issues must be addressed: the nature of the human and the nature of the Spirit, the destiny, how it is perceived, both human and spiritual. What is important to the human will not be important to the Spirit. What the human finds subjective and personal, the Spirit will find objective and impersonal. We also have bodies that can't hold dreams and they give up because they're prancing around their territory. They've got to keep moving to keep their boundaries safe. And we have a God who is endeavoring to get the experience through.

When you choose to have a life to where you dedicate it to your spiritual revelation, you are asking for a life in which you must ride those horses of the sensual self with a tight rein. And in this life the Spirit must be developed and the painful process of taking back one's power often means tripping up the body, its family roots, and pulling out from under it its own rug of blame and jealousy, the dynamics of family situations, pulling the rug out from under sexuality, pulling the rug out from under prejudice and saying in an unequal yet singular tone, "I created this. It never was your fault. I made you think it was your fault because that's the coward in me. I blamed you for the *lessness* I feel about myself when it had nothing to do with you. I inflicted the lack of self-love upon me and indeed it is I who have rejected myself and cloistered myself. I am the one who left you. You never left me. I am the one who has wallowed in self-pity and *languored* in my past. You never were in my present because I was never there. I was gone. I was in yesterday. It's not your fault. It's just a habit I have."

It takes great spiritual depth to be an honorable man and an honorable woman, and it hurts deeply. But rather than feeling hurt, feel the coming back of the wind of begotten energy moving through the emotional body and purifying it to make us whole rather than never having been whole at all.

And when we were last together I talked to you about intense clarity, pure and unobstructed, and this is what I am talking about. And that every thought is minted out decisively. It is never simply taken for randomness, but it is contemplated so much so until the extraordinary and lofty way to think becomes the common way to think. That's hard to do, especially when your body tells you you're missing a lot. And it's hard to stay in the dark night of the soul without stimulus to get you out of it. But why would you want to get you out of it? It's pulling that energy back from those painful places that must pass through the emotional body. That's where the true suffering is, but that is also where purification is. To dull it, to get rid of it, would deny yourself purification and thus wisdom.

So be it.

II.
One Fine Morning

O my beloved God,
unto me this day
move as my holy Spirit,
to draw me up
into your realm
and hold me there.
O my beloved God,
let my Spirit
flow from my being
unencumbered.
I accept this knowledge
in freedom.
I desire
its revelation
unto me.
O my beloved God,
I am thankful
for my life.
O my beloved God,
I am thankful
for my body.
My beloved God,
fill me with your love
eternally,
and God bless my life.
So be it.

To life.

Now let's do a little review. We want to evolve to a deeper knowledge, the knowledge that we had, and set our mind on a righteous path to understanding.

Now the first teaching I gave you, you chose to be here, to come here, and to learn a spiritual understanding. No one made you come here. You're here because this is what you want to learn. Self-choice is the beginning of self-empowerment or the redefinition of self.

Now what was the second thing? Defining self. Now we're still a little hazy here about self, and it's only a term. And these words that I use, they are only words. What's important is reminding you of the two evenings [4] that we had together in your time where I talked about learning to hear and why it was important that a master teach you, teach you because if you are hearing, it is causing what to occur in your brain? Pictures, holograms. That's the way to hear.

These words stimulate the brain to create pictures. And as you also learned, that true self is imagination. It's the act of imaging. That's our destiny; that's what we're supposed to do.

So if you listen today or you are reading my words, it will help to redefine perhaps old definitions because as I talk and if you can stay with me, your brain is going to produce the pictures that my words, properly placed, are going to occur in your brain. And if they do, then you are now thinking in spiritual terms.

The definition of self. We must go all the way back then to Point Zero, to what I taught when you first came to see me: You are God. And then of course we have to redefine what God is and remove from it the shackles of limitation and dogma. And we use that which is termed physics to be able to explain the metamorphosis of involution as well as evolution, reality. Self is a pure creative state of consciousness and its handmaiden energy, inextricably combined; that's what we really, really are. And that self creating is none other than the godhead itself. That's what we are.

---

[4] Previously held Advanced Evening Events "Crossing the River Part 1" and "Crossing the River Part 2," currently available to students who have achieved the Level 2 Retreat.

If we understand then that we are not really the faces that we wear and we're not really the garment that we wear and, moreover, we really aren't the territories that we define, then we start to see self in its most pure origin when we understand that self is not the subjective body that we exist in, but that it is the inactive mind of one of all reality. With this brain that has the ability to contemplate the infinite, even on its finite terms, you begin to see then that our spiritual self has been a rolling culmination of the very experiences that it created.

Now listen to what I said, that the Spirit is the rolling culmination of the very experiences that it has created in its eons of manifestation. So what that means then is essentially the self is a broad mind — a mind, really — a mind that is made up of all of its consciousness and energy that it created. And that to move through a creation and not finish it would be a fracturing of that self. And remember that's what we are. And we then as consciousness and energy, the godhead itself, have only one real destiny, and that is to make known the unknown. And the more that we do so, to imagine the unimaginable, the greater our unity as God as oneness becomes. That's what we're supposed to do. We are an ocean seeping into the shores of the Void and we should be expanding that which we are. That's what the self is.

If we are then an enigma, a mystifying etherical quality called consciousness and energy, then the soul is what captures and holds forever the final experience, the final movement of that experience. And it is the soul and the holding of that experience in its finality that allows consciousness to be so broad. Without the soul helping to define mind, we would only be creating, moving through the creation. And as soon as we've moved through it, we're back where we were originally because we have no margin — we have created no margin — of static reality of which to build other concepts from.

Here we have then the soul of memorable experience within the conscious energy self. It's the quality that allows our mind to grow and to expand. It gives us our finished business to which we use as springboards to create the next unimaginable. Now that's self, and it's awesome and powerful.

When we know that about what we are, we can see then clearly why a life pursued, coming out of the wilderness and out of the murk and the mire, a life that is born here in which the pursuit of destiny and goal of that life is to find out what we are, is the loftiest life we'll ever live. Because when we begin to imagine ourselves — not in the eyes of humanity — but when we begin to define ourselves in much broader terms, unimaginable terms, we start to locate what we are. That is the discovery of who we are. It's time to take a look at what is true and real about ourself. That we call the spiritual life. That is the spiritual life.

Now to define ourself. What we learned then was that self is in the body of an incarnation like yours; that self, when it was in the Plane of Bliss last time and every time from prior incarnations, arrived there at heaven. The great agenda there, the great judgment day, the hour of judgment, is to see for ourselves both subjective and objective those aspects of how we placed energy and how ultimately we affected this central core of our being — past life review, as you like to call it in its flowery cosmic terms.

And what is important about that is that in this hour of judgment there is no one there in heaven, in Bliss, that is the judge. What we are is ourself. And we have found then that what covers up self is unfinished business. We learned a term called encumbrance, to be encumbered. When we viewed then our past life and what you're going to do in this one, you're going to see everything. There is nothing that was ever forgotten in energy because every act was preceded by a thought and that is what is real. The thought is real because it is what self is. It is consciousness and energy. So we review what is real. And nothing is wasted.

And we see everything that we did, what we thought we were doing behind closed doors or behind the placid face of indifference or smiling emptiness. We begin to see it not only as we who did it and were thinking it, but consciousness and energy from this point of view as self are both. So we not only get to see subjectively what we were thinking, but we also get to feel it subjectively as energy and where it was headed. Because we are, as we have learned, one, that God is one mind. So what we do, we do to ourself, regardless of the players. The players are ourself. Because that's how large self is.

And we learned that in doing to someone else, we have done to ourself. In victimizing and being unmerciful, uncaring, entrapping, enslaving, being decadent, being uncharitable, being unforgiving, we've done to ourself. So in the light review, we get to feel what that feels like. Well, everything is energy and therefore we are the creators of that energy. Then it is our expulsion of that energy that comes home to us. That's judgment day.

And why is it a painful moment? We learned, because we really get to see every facet of ourself and we see the dynamics of that facet, that we become the injured that we have injured. We become the enslaved that we enslaved. We are the victims of our abuse. And we feel it on every corner. We also learned why that's important is because in order to do any of these acts in a lifetime, we must have a divine quality that we can utilize to do it with. In other words, no act again is not preceded by a thought, and the thought is coming from the divine source inside of us. So the act is us. We learned then, remembering that, that our encumbrances are giving our power away, fracturing our God, and being unwhole.

Defining self in the spiritual life is about being in pursuit of the knowledge that allows us to address our encumbrances. It allows us in the spiritual life to find out who we are. It is important that we do so. We never walk as angels in the beginning of this spiritual journey. We come humbly with our dead mules at the door, our hauntings, our phantoms, our sufferings, our anxieties. And the devil that we bring with us is our *altered* ego.

We learn then that the spiritual life is about taking power back. Of everything I've taught you, the essential message is regaining coherently the power that you have fractured away because when you do, you dismantle the temple within; you dismantle the godhood within. And every block, every golden stone that makes up the temple of the self, has been given to all of these particular areas that constitute an inordinate amount of suffering because we are separated from our God because our God is fractured around us. That is an encumbrance.

In order then to do the unimaginable, we have to rebuild this temple. We have to redefine ourself and that's not easy. And many of you contemplated about — really true and sincere contemplation — where have you given your power away and what does that mean. And that doesn't mean giving it to somebody to control your life, although that's an aspect of it. It doesn't really mean that; it's a finer, more mystical meaning. It means holding onto your past.

You see, the fracturing of God as encumbrances is only locked up in the past. That is what it's locked up at. And we addressed this, the victims of your past experiences. A chronic one in this audience is that you've been abused by your parents, or you were ignored by your parents, or you were abandoned by your parents, and that you move through life with this sickening attitude of lack and that you point the finger at them, him or her — and these are examples — or to your friend or someone who abused you, or to someone who took advantage of you, or someone who pulled the rug out from under you. You go through life pointing fingers. "It's their fault I'm this way." That's the fracturing of self because what that means is that instead of taking responsibility for creating this — which is what God is about; God is the creator and, I tell you, that's what you are — that instead of taking the responsibility of that, which will define self, you fracture it by pointing fingers and saying, "They did this to me and I was innocent." No one is innocent. And the moment that you do and you create tyrants in your life, then you have taken part of the temple and you've set it over there, and its reality and its dynamic are to do this to you. And as we also learned, it's so tempting from the human point of view to be the victim, because everyone is. The social consciousness of capitalism is to be victimized so that they can find ways to get you out of it temporarily. It's easy, because it's much easier to say, "I am the way I am because of this and that," people, places, things, times, and events. And when you do, it works for a while.

And look how you've used it. You've used it to excuse the lack of strength. You've used it to excuse your illness. You have used it to cleverly bind people to you through their sympathy and empathy. You have used it to get your way. It has served you. You are a capitalist. That's what you are.

And no one really wants to give that up because, as we also learned, the animal in you, the survivalist with definable boundaries, the herdlike creature, that creature demands survival. And if every one of you stop serving the herd, what happens is the moment you say "I created it." — I; I is God — "I created it. This is my own creation." — the moment you do that, you remove your power from your parents, people, places, things, times, and events. You remove it from there and you start to rebuild the temple in here; and that — as we also learned, and you have contemplated about — is a very painful process. The dark night of the soul is when we finally take responsibility for our actions. And what happens then is the energy that is coming home from poor mom and dad — and remember they're just Gods too — the energy that is coming home from your brother and your sister or your husbandman, your wife, or your relationship, when you start to take responsibility, look how consciousness works. Because if it is that and it has control of energy, when you take "I" from out there and put it back in here, then the energy starts to dissolve from mom and dad and it starts moving back to you, and it's passing through those bands. It's coming home.

Now the dark night of the soul is when the energy rushes through the emotional body. In other words, it was once sent out through the emotional body as feeling, was it not, to create. Remember we have learned that? So now it's going to come back home and impact the same feeling. That is only when energy becomes purified is when it enters back into the physical realm of the emotional body. Simply said, when you take your power back of making someone else your tyrants, then the energy starts coming back to you in the form of a tyrant. That energy is a thought form, it's tyrannical, and it hits the emotional body, and it's like a reverse charge. Instead of the energy coming from here and being affected hormonally, it's coming from out there, passing through the energy band and hitting the body as a direct charge. It's a reverse charge into the brain. When it does, it activates the field and it causes suffering. This is where tears come from. This is where wailing comes from. This is where anguish comes from. And if someone says to you, "What is wrong with you?" "I don't know." Well, this is what it is: Your chickens are coming home to roost.

Now this is very hard to do because I've taught you so much to have joy, and I will continue to teach you to do that, but we must be free of our encumbrances. What we started we must complete, and we must bring the energy back to the temple here and we have to build it within ourself. That is the self; that's redefining it and it's painful. No one wants to take responsibility for something that all these years has served them so well. They don't want to take responsibility that really they're the one that lived in the past of a circumstance and that the people who were connected have long gone. Nobody wants to admit that that's how they lived their life. It's hard.

But when energy passes through the dark night of the soul, then it's home and the self starts to be defined. This is pure judgment. And I tell you something I did not tell you last evening that will become self-evident through this workshop is that the spiritual path is the path of purging and it is the path of cleansing. It is nothing about cleansing the body or the colon. It is not. I am not speaking in those terms. I have to be very clear.

Ascension. To ascend in a lifetime without death is the marvelous opportunity that happens through an absolutely pure and impassioned spiritual life. Let's look at it. Let's look at it for a moment, shall we? We are getting rid of our encumbrances. We're finishing them, aren't we? And as we finish them, we also learned that in heaven, that Plane of Bliss where we were in the rooms of contemplation, we imagined how we were going to finish it. We were going to, in very base terms, make it all right. And I taught you how elaborate that can be. In heaven, in the Plane of Bliss, it's instantaneous, and imagination is the natural order of the self. It happens instantly. So we work to form a life and attract the proper players in that life so that we can. Our object is to do that.

So now having reminded you of that, in the Plane of Bliss we labor here as a spiritual life that in one lifetime we are to resolve our encumbrances, to move through the experiences, and define self all the way. And the more that we take the responsibility for our actions, no matter how painful, the more powerful we become.

Now remember we're still in one lifetime here, perhaps this lifetime. And we work to resolve them. That is the labor of this existence. And there will come one fine morn when you will wake up free. And what is it that you're free from? I tell you maybe thousands of lifetimes of trying to resolve the same encumbrance because, try as we may in heaven, we are cowards in the flesh on the hard and difficult road of the spiritual path. Suddenly one morning we wake up and it's in this lifetime and it's done. We wake up from our beds before dawn and go and look out that frosted window pane and watch Ra as it ascends in the sky, and we truly understand this is the moment of all eternity. "I am free. That freedom means I am clear. I am absolutely purged of my shattered self. I have reclaimed the power of my being. I have no shadows. I am purified." And it is the moment of restoration. And it is the finest moment; it is one fine morn. We are free. And we are free of endeavoring to do this for lifetimes. Such joy in that moment.

One day you'll have your morning and you will understand what I am endeavoring to tell you. Now that is the fruit of the spiritual work.

What happens after that is that line of potential that you created the unimaginable imagined starts to then, with clarity, move into your life. There is nothing stopping what you created in heaven from being manifested here. There is no ulterior motive, that the future created on the Plane of Bliss cannot be stopped because we have encumbered ourself from our past. And we're clear and we're clean and we have been purged and we're whole. The self has been reestablished. It's been reborn. The temple has been rebuilt. We have Christ emerging in the self. And every time we did, we gained more strength, more spiritual power, little by little by little. And this morning we are free of our past, utterly and cleanly. We are no one's child, except ourself. And then that wild potential that we created in Bliss starts to manifest because we're clean. We're in the moment; we're in the present. And what we created that we wish to do falls into place effortlessly.

But how wise are we after this? We have understood clearly that in giving our power away, interrupting the free will of someone else, blaming the will of someone else, destroying our own, we have learned a valuable lesson. We have lived long enough in one life of one memory to be able to reconcile it in the flesh. And it is here that we must do it because it is the roots of the kingdom of heaven, and the root is what nourishes the leaves on the top, and here we are.

And what does that mean then? When that fine morning comes, we do not have to do a light review. What is to review? There is nothing to review. And then is it possible then that time stops? It does, because the clock of time runs in past thinking. It stops in the present; that's when it stops.

Now we ascend from a life that starts out as spiritual unencumbering. We are starting to walk the pathways of a master. The master then is one who walks to rebuild this. Regardless of this, it is rebuilding this. And when it is done, we have a full flowering of that master. We have total power. Now understand what that means, people. What is the difference between you and a full-blown God, a full-blown master? The difference is that you are fractured in every aspect of your life: You have blamed, you have put upon, you have used, you have abused, you have done all of the things that are not right and wrong. But what they have done is that they have crippled your ability to do the extraordinary, haven't they? Because doing the extraordinary means that we must come back to the temple of

God and be a God so that when we lay our word out, the word is manifested straightaway, like it is in Bliss. The difference between you is that they are together; they have defined the self. And your self is scattered all over the place; it's everywhere. They have defined it, but they labored to define it.

Now there is no such death for such a being. You know why? Because they are fully loaded with the godhead. Their bodies will be transmuted by the enormous amount of radioactive energy being asserted from that godhead, that most powerful place. You think that the splitting of one minute atom can set off a rage of devastation, but it is nothing compared to the energy that emanates from the godhead. Now what has flesh to do with such a powerhouse? It's going to be saved by it. The body will be able to be transmuted and it doesn't have to go to the worm. What grace, and it is a natural evolution.

It's not that the master ever stops and thinks about it. You know, every day you're thinking about your body. A master doesn't do that. It doesn't even do that. Because in doing that therein lies giving your power away. Understand? Well, you could argue, "Where is the fine line in taking care of yourself?" That's self. If we take care of that, it will take care of everything else. There is no time for a master. What you read about the great masters of the Far East and the Far West is true. Their answers boggle your mind, they're so simple. And your animal trashes them because it tries to figure it out and interpret it and, you know, it never will. These are the answers of the Spirit; they're not the answers of the body. They're the answers of the Spirit. They're talking to you from self. That's the language of self.

"In one fine moment I realized what I was." My God, that's a baptism in fire. They're telling you the truth. "In one fine moment I realized what I was." Well, what was it that they realized? They were God. And you can't be God and be a victim. Who is God to be victim to? Who is God to be hurt by? Who is God to be limited by? Do you understand? Now these are the blocks. But in one fine moment they had the capacity to realize that, my beautiful people, and it all came home to them. It all came home to them.

And what happened? They stopped aging. We age only because we keep echoing the past forward. And how is that possibly connected? Because the emotional patterns of the hard-wiring up here keeps reminding us of what we are not, and that past is an emotional body.

Now energy between two points of consciousness is defining time, its velocity, its momentum; that is defining time. Now we have two levels of consciousness in this body. We have body-mind consciousness and we have God consciousness; therefore time bounces back and forth between the two. But if we then take that and understand it as a momentum, the body is continuously under emotional duress; and that means that if it is, the emotions that are moving from within the body are draining the storehouses of hormones and energy that govern them. And those fundamental building blocks of the tangible physical are being used up every day by reminding ourself of something that we used to get away with in our youth but has taken its toll in middle age. So every day the emotional trauma of your past eats away, and that is time. That's why when the encumbrances of the past are owned and the power is taken back, the past reaction ceases. Do you understand?

Getting back to ascension. All ascension becomes is the natural apogee for owning one's encumbrances. The master truly is walking on the face of the earth at this point.

Now why are they staying? If they've owned all of their encumbrances, then why stick around? What they have never been able to do for lifetimes is enjoy a timeless life. Isn't that beautiful? A timeless life. And also to have the freedom in a body to be what they were on the Plane of Bliss, to imagine the unimaginable and make it happen instantaneously. Isn't that what we're sticking around for, to see what we could do with that? Oh, absolutely. And they gauge themselves and they know that when it doesn't happen instantaneously, there is a little light that's going off, an alarm sounding upstairs. And what is the alarm telling them if it doesn't happen instantaneously? They're fractured. Very nice.

It is possible in one lifetime to do it all. The masters then enjoy a timeless life, and then their great work starts to come out of them at that point. And when they find that instantaneously what they have imagined doesn't happen, they have learned then that there is a slight fracture in their godhead and they absolutely know what it is, and they have understood then that in some point they have given their power away at some place. And they have to root it out and they find it. That's a master. Do you understand?

It becomes simple to understand then that the walk of the master is a solitary life. It's solitude, solitary, but can be shared by many masters. And why do I say this? I say this because each individual entity has to construct its own reality. And in constructing its own reality, that reality can be shared by many masters, but the master itself is a sovereign, an individual being that has not given any power away, only in terms of lending its support. And it enjoys the company of other masters because there is an equilibrium; there is a balance in their community.

You'll never hear a master recant its past. You'll never hear a master talk about another entity. You'll never hear a master hold itself less than anyone else. But by the same token you also get the distinctive feeling that they're greatly humble. They are. They don't have an *altered* ego. And they're shamelessly humble but all-powerful. And they don't meddle in the affairs of men; they don't meddle in the affairs of women. They understand and, rightfully so, what the path is all about. And they are not going to interfere in your life. No one interferes in your life because if you're God, you've got to ask, and only then do you have intervention or help. They don't do that.

So why do the masters stay away from you? What do you bring to the table? What do you bring to their table? You are not yet the unimaginable imagined. So what do you bring to the table except a whining need to have someone else do it for you. And do you know you can ask their help and they can make the phenomenon happen. But are they going to continue the phenomenon? Are they going to splinter their energy and let you ride on it for the rest of your life? The minute they draw it back, what happens to the rider? They fall, don't they? They're not going to do that because they know that that's worse than any cripple there ever was.

S o the true spiritual life then is about a life that we are born into to understand self and to heal it and to make a life dedicated to the art of healing it. And what begins to happen that's so different than the group across the river that is inventing computers is that the spiritual life is an eternal one, so that when we do heal it, we belong to the ages; we belong to eternity. When we focus on what has given us life and what we truly are and we endeavor to become it and understand its methodology and its science, the mechanics of how it works, when we dedicate a life to doing that, then that Spirit is our reward in a never-ending existence.

We touched on understanding this but we didn't touch on ascension. The masters, what happens to them? Well, they never die. And I have just explained to you through pure logic how that is possible and why it is possible.

So now I say to you, my beloved people, what enemy do you have that is worth eternal life? And what lack do you hold on so aggressively to as to miss ascension? What resentment do you harbor that hereto has served you in a pitiful realm? Is it really worth losing a life of unimaginable dynamics for?

There becomes a very clear distinction between the *altered* ego and the defining self. Analogical mind is a constant. And that when we own the past and our encumbrances, we have clarity. And it isn't even a question about doubting. There is no doubt in the godhead. How could God doubt itself? It doesn't. On the other side of encumbrances lies the unimaginable and lie the possibilities of the unimaginable to be instantaneous. We're really fast. But if fast is broken up into attitudes, we're slow. God is fractured in the attitude. God is fractured in the body. We can't do it so we think it's impossible. Well, isn't that an excuse.

One fine morning that feeling of unbelievable joy when it is accomplished is the joy you're going to have. And it will be constant because there's nothing tugging on you anymore, there's nothing eating on you anymore, there's nothing that you have to do. You've cleaned your house.

It takes ten million lifetimes sometimes to clean up one attitude. Or it can take one life focused on doing that to clean them all out and then never die and then walk with Gods because you bring to the table your sovereignty, your dignity, and your power. That's what gives you power.

Now the reason it is so important is because that's what we did on the Plane of Bliss. That's what we learned to do on Bliss, that in a moment there was nothing that stood in the way of our imagination. Everything obeys because we're closer in the triad. On the third, fourth, and fifth planes we are closer to the godhead. Our vibration is instantaneous. And yet we still have the sixth and the seventh to go. How much more rapid does that become?

That's how we really are. We really are this creature who has a propensity for imagination because that is its natural order and that imagination instantly is collapsed into tangible form. And here we are creatures, Gods, in all our splendor, who keep fracturing ourself for silly, fruitless games that just postpone the owning of it all, what was supposed to be simply an experience of evolution, and we throw it away. When we have parted the curtains long enough and held them at bay, our instantaneous mind comes forward. That's who you really are. That is the entity that in the spiritual life we desire to be at all times.

Now this school is defining that self, defining it. We only make it hard on ourself. Isn't that an interesting phrase? Hard on self. It takes on a new light, does it not?
What was the third thing that you learned? You learned in the orientation about going to the light and the day of judgment and you learned about being all things in that light review, the subject as well as the observer.

And we learned then that after we have this life review, as troubling as it is, we are nonetheless closer to our natural element in Bliss than we are here in this foreign land. And therein we have a place to which we can go into contemplation. And we learned about the different areas of contemplation: pizza parlors on the fourth plane, sitting by a great and beautiful placid lake, instantly appearing, sitting in the midst of the Void somewhere. We call it the halls of contemplation — now this is important — in which we have the ability of contemplation. We have now been removed out of our *altered* ego.

We can retain the likeness of our former body if we wish to help to remind us what we need to do, but we've been removed from it. We don't really care who we left behind anymore. And we don't really care about what went on with our personal property after our death. We really don't care. As much as the lawyers tell you, we don't care. And we really are very different than what we were in that human existence. But we're close to the existence because we have to now go and, taken from what we gained from that existence, we have to be able to contemplate knowing that contemplation is our natural order because as soon as we do, it appears. We must contemplate on how to finish the business that in yet another lifetime we were unable to do.

And we all know when we're in that place how cowardly the body is, the human is. We know that. And how do we yet move into that orb of experience and be able to impress what we want upon a brain that clearly is not going to remember? Now as long as we understand the unity, God-is-one, then the sweet things of our life are going to be carried on genetically. If we bore children in that life, then one honorable thing that will happen is that we've started a bloodline to which we helped produce. And here is the advantage of that. We know that our attitudes become flesh in the next generation. And what better place would we want to land then and work on unfinished business but in the very genetic pool that we're endeavoring to address concurrently.

So in this place we are endeavoring to figure out that line of potential and create our future, to be able to finish this business up. Because again let me tell you it's not about being a good person or a bad person; it is about what we do with opportunities and with which level of consciousness. Do we approach them with the human that is instinctively a coward, or do we approach them with the Spirit that is all-prevailing? It is about creating, experiencing, so that the soul has yet another block, another tool to build another reality based upon that wisdom. That's why it's so important.

We know all of this, but we know that our unfinished business, as we learned, can never be finished in Bliss. Oh, we can see the end of it. Why, we can see what we are in other realms. We get the opportunity to play there. We get the opportunity to instantly see what we would be if we were this life or that life or some other life. You understand? We are only limited to what we know. And we get to do all of that. We can take our next incarnation and we can go all the way through. We can visualize for ourselves the most idealistic life, but it isn't really going to happen for us. We're not going to gain the substance of the wisdom unless we come back to the place of its origin, down here, the plane of demonstration, the thick, gooey, syrupy plane. This is where we have to be defined at and we have to make known it here.

So how do we transfer our sublime and sparkling consciousness that immediately imagines and it is? How can we get that magic into that body? Well, we know that the only way we can get it there is if we lay a course ahead of time on Bliss of what we want to have accomplished down here. Now how are we going to get into it? Well, we're going to permeate the bands that surround the tissue of the child in the womb. The child in the womb is going to feed off of those bands. But more importantly we've laid the program in the soul, the one who remembers. And the soul is what is going to give life to child in utero. The soul is going to create the rhythmic beating of the heart. Because it (the soul) is called the lord of the body, it also has jurisdiction over how the genes play a part in manufacturing the body. It's going to do that. But it is not going to make the brain have memory of which it does not yet have. Do you understand? It can only store it away in the lower cerebellum. That's the only place it's allowed to store it.

We know that when we're in Bliss. We learned then at this place that we do have the body factor to consider, but how about players? We learned about the people who are going to play the parts. One important teaching that we gained is that not everyone that we've met in this life means that we've met them in previous incarnations. To think that way is to think strictly linear. That is unenlightened. How about multidimensional? That's much more expansive than basing a familiarity on a time line that's long and flat.

We learned that not everyone that we know or feel familiar with we ever shared an experience with before. They are our future. And we also learned that the way that we understand that is that if — and following the logic of the teaching — everyone goes through the life review except the masters, then everybody's being processed, aren't they, on Bliss. And they're all coming in from all nations, all countries, and all worlds. And they're coming into their particular sector, aren't they? And they're all coming in having to face their encumbrances. And they all get a rest period to rest. They all need it. Everyone needs it. I needed it.

And then they get to see what they were. They get to see the life that is only an unwinding of their own consciousness. And everything is remembered because we gave power to everything. Every thought is a thing. We get to see it real and tangible. Well, if that isn't exhausting, I don't know what is.

And so then we are all given ages in which to contemplate if we want to heal. Healing doesn't mean that we're suffering on Bliss. We don't suffer on Bliss. Healing is to heal the bruising of our subjective/objective self, to finish business up.

So in these rooms of contemplation we learned that in turning to your partner and sharing conversation, you're sharing ideas. If you're really listening, if you're listening to your partner, their mind is now causing your mind to fire. So you're getting to walk through their mind, aren't you? That's conversation. And then when you come back and you talk, before you can say the word, the picture is formed up here. When you say the word, the person then gets to take a walk through your mind. But most people are very poor at sharing. But for the most part that's how it works. On Bliss, when we start to contemplate, it isn't that we talk. We don't talk. We think, if you will. We have thoughts. We image.

That's our communiqué. And as we're imaging a time line and figuring out, plotting and planning, on how to resolve suffering, how to resolve victimization, how to heal hate, this is all unfinished business. We're actually seeing those pictures greater than three or four dimensions and in the most unbelievable colors. And what happens is other people who move into that area – and there are a lot of people there — and they move into that area and they're imaging too.

And we're always drawn to our likeness. When we evolve we will drop away our unlikeness and evolve to our next likeness. So it's possible, let's say, for example, as we learn that in the dappled wood there is a great community that happened to enjoy the features of the forest, and there they are creating and letting it float across a crystal lake their line potential, and they're getting to do that. And there is an entity seated, if you will, a few feet away. And they seem to have a very similar problem they're working on. So you know how we communicate? We image together, just like you do, like I'm getting you trained to do. We image together.

And what happens is you may have met up with someone from the sixth dimension who still has an issue, and it may not be in the same dynamics yours is, but it's a dynamic that has to do with fracturing. Do you understand? And they may be sitting right beside you. And what happens, your potential lines start blending with one another and you're exactly what they need and they are exactly what you need. Are you with me? Now we could say that that's a real partnership born in heaven. Well, it is; it really is. And you have never ever met this entity before, but it's where minds came to meet and therein lies the sharing.

So what happens is that when both of you have an approval on that, it's inevitable you're going to meet again because for that line potential to manifest, it takes that entity to appear. Now we learned that.

In groups, you could be sitting with a whole gabby group. It looks like a circus. And they're all meeting to work out a group problem that they think they individually had, but as it turns out many in the section had it, didn't they? And they all had different areas of the fracture and they start imagining, and pretty soon the whole picture comes together and it starts to flow and everyone gets what they want. Now that is a group from heaven that come and meet along the way.

They could be born in the great north, the far south. They could be born into abject poverty; they could be born into riches. They can be black, yellow, white, green, or gray; it doesn't matter. They came here with a soul destiny and they are going to be magnetized. As they move in their life, if they are able to accomplish this, they are going to meet up together because as they approach the hour when the test is on, that the test now is unfolding in the drama of your life, suddenly you start to meet them, and immediately the test is on and they can come from everywhere. This is in reality great beings that share a healing on another level that are here, and they come together and you meet with them or you are them or you enjoin with them or you're with them for a time.

And, you know, that's when the Spirit is at war with the flesh because in this, this is clearly a button being pushed for the spiritual's line of potential to occur now in which the actual healing happens. And these beings were together before this incarnation. It isn't what do you have in common as far as gold and what you have in common as far as youth. You don't have anything physical in common but you have a great deal at that time, on that time line, in common. You are there to facilitate a healing, a restoration, if you will, of a fractured God of unfinished business. Got it?

When the healing happens, the group splits up and goes their way. Why can't they do that? Why can't you let them do that? Why can't you understand that people are going to pass in and out of your life and that when you came together, you came together for something to occur. Growth is what it's called. Why do you hold onto them when the growth has been accomplished? They've served a purpose. It's over with. That was the purpose. You served them; they served you. The clinging nature of human beings is to cling and to hold onto, to build territories and boundaries around; that's the animal. When you let go, then you're finished and you don't generate a past, do you? Because if you hold onto it, you keep the wound open. Do you understand? We're there to meet, to heal, to go on.

We also talked about people in heaven or in Bliss who meet up with each other, and the dynamics of likeness are so profound that love is actually generated there, a deep abiding, rich love. Now I've taught you about love. Love is pure God. Love is the act of pure giving. God is not a taker; God is a giver. And that love is the cosmic glue that holds all things together. It is possible that in these areas of contemplation that two beings come together that are so much alike, that the healing is actually, instead of the one, the healing of the two as one. And that dynamic between them is called love.

They have no lack. There is no lack. When there is no lack, there is love. And they came together and had none at all. And when they came down here to tend to their business, the other one followed and they searched their life to find one another. And they know that when their business is done, they'll come together because that was a promise they made.

So I'm going to ask you: Do you know what that is on the other side of your encumbrances? Who awaits you on the other side? Who awaits you that one fine morning? What awaits to come into your life that hereto has not been there?

And we also talked about beings who come together here and find the same rare bonding. Now that bonding is what God is all about. They are one. They represent a wholeness. Love is not fractured; it is whole. It is *unfractureable*. It is the radiating energy of wholeness. That is why masters are filled with love, because they are whole.

If I tell you then that the fracturing of God is out in your enemies and I tell you that your enemies are as important to you as those that you love — because your God lives in them in your mind — when we rebuild the self, what kind of radiation is this energy? It's total love because it has no lack.

Now we have you and I in our lives, and some of you have found that rarefied being that when unified had no lack, none. So when there is no lack, there is a radiance of love. Those beings have found true God and oneness and healed. It is the way we all wish to be. It is only with love that we can bring forth the unimaginable. We can never bring forth the unimaginable in lack.

We learned that those entities, when one passes, they'll wait for the other one in the gardens of contemplation. And when they come back, it's a *rejoyful* reunion. Or if we see that during their life it was cut short and they come back, the other will wait for them because, you see, that love was an unexpected in their life. It happened. It was one of those clear, lucid moments that allowed it to slip in to know and to be and to feel. And they returned to the garden, and they won't come back to life until their love comes back. We get that choice.

We also learned that our enemies usually agree to be our enemies in the garden of contemplation because they've got to have a victim. We learned then by looking at this, that this is nothing more than a gigantic play. It is. And every move and every line count. And the stage is always changing. The opportunities are always changing. We understand that when we pass to the other side, we really don't have any malice for anyone, so why should we have them here? If that then is the case, then wouldn't that be the true spiritual life?

So what is being a spiritual person about? It is about being the self, utterly and totally, that the self is all things and all beings. And that the self, if who we want to be is spiritual, we will never ever hold a grudge against anyone because if we don't do it in Bliss and we have instantaneous manifestation, why do we insist on doing it here? And, second, that we should forgive everyone because in doing so, we forgive ourself. In forgiving ourself, we take the monkey off of our back and give the power back to us. When we learn that everyone is us, in the way that we are, then we're being spiritual because why can we not be on earth as we are in heaven. We simply have to choose to be it and we have to look at the conditions of being it. If there is no cheating in heaven, why do we do it here? And if there's no doubting in heaven, why do we insist on doing it here? If there is no malice in heaven, why do we insist on doing it here? Are you beginning to understand?

III.
Resolution

To more freedom.
Isn't it so, that the truth does set you free?
It does.
God, let us always wish for that freedom.
So be it.

To life.

Now what was then the next thing, the next point, that we learned? Resolution. A very nice word. Sort of sounds like revolution, a spiritual revolt.

Now already we have discussed today in review what unfinished business is. And although I have put out some very harsh examples, it is the irony that those are the examples that are always put forward because, as I have said to you, there are things about our life that will always be with us. They are the sweet things; they are the true godhead. Those are the great acts that we do that really transcend the normal course of business. There are aspects of ourself that we've earned the right to be defined by. And these aspects, as in human consciousness, we could say, well, those are the good things. Well, they are the virtuous things, they are the virtuous lessons, they're the virtuous deeds. Now there are things about aspects, about colors, about dimensions, to all of you here that are really quite spectacular and that you've earned the right to keep those. Those are not disingenuous to your nature; they're quite genuine. And those we don't need to talk about because when we do acts, when we impart the extraordinary from ourself, we are not fracturing; we are defining. And those qualities all of you have.

At some point in your life you have been called upon by a friend or a desperate neighbor, or in a time of chaos and misery, that something greater has risen out of you and you have acquiesced. Now these are the great defining qualities in our life that will never be taken away from us because they echo what God is. And you know, my beloved people, there are certainly many incidents in nature or through intentional human destruction that all of you have been participants to.

And whereas only days before you may have been griping and complaining about your neighbors — because, like I told you last night, there are stinkers in this group and you know who you are — but isn't it interesting how the humanity part of us is quick to recognize that in someone else because that's what is in ourself, isn't it? That's where our energy is, isn't it? That's the fracturing of us. And then the next day a terrible incident could befall those neighbors in a very, perhaps, life- threatening way and suddenly, without even thinking, we are riveted from our comfort zone of conceit and arrogance and we are transported into a venue of thought that seems to spring from somewhere deep inside of us, and we rush to their aid and we help. We hold back the waters; we move the food. We take *raggedy* smelly children in our arms and, where two days before we couldn't tolerate the sight of blood, we are there cleaning wounds, holding them dear to our breast where our soul lives. And we're helping. And when two days before we were complaining about our lack of revenue or lack of funds, suddenly it doesn't even become an issue. Your hand reaches for your pocketbook and you pull it out and you give, and you don't even think about the consequences of giving.

Now that is our nature, our true defining moments of self. And that when we do help, no matter the cost — and sometimes the greater the call, which would demand of you the greater the cost, the greater the effort — it's in those moments that we are defined as God. We truly are. Or as some historians would say then, those are the defining moments, the crowning jewel of human existence.

These are the great points about us. There's not one of you that really hasn't in a small or a large way riveted from the hypocrite to the God in a matter of moments. Those kindnesses, those thoughtfulnesses, those areas of generosity without thought to the repercussion to yourself, when you do that, you're God. When you pause and reflect and think, then you redefine your boundaries and the moment passes, and that defining of God has missed its opportunity.

This act of emergency that we arise to is what helps to not only define the self but it also binds us to the eternal self. Now these are the great things that we have done, you know? Someone who loses their purse and has all of their life savings in it and you, who are working on fabulous wealth, find it, it is a great temptation to say that it is your manifestation. That is the altered human instinct to survive. The honorable God, without question,

68

would find its rightful owner because in that rarefied moment we are back on the Plane of Bliss because, you see, on the Plane of Bliss there is no need; there is only the expansion of knowledge to make greater forms of preexistence. That's when the God kicks in. That's when we are at our best. That's when we are at our most ennobled.

Those great acts say that if the bread truck breaks down on the way to market, and we've been without bread for three days, does not necessarily mean it's ours. There is an impeccable and unimpeachable quality that will always arise in us that we'll do our best, hungry as we are, to make certain that the bread arrives safely to its destination. Now isn't that the way a master thinks? Wouldn't that be the way they would think? Absolutely. Then we get to experience in those moments really our spiritual self and we get to see who we are. And it floods us with a generosity of feeling that makes us feel wonderful. Well, only the Spirit can flood us with that sort of joy, that sort of feeling that picks us up out of the murk and mire of survival because God is a giver. And in that moment we are God back in the temple, in that splendid moment.

Those are the things that are precious about you, all of you, standing up for your neighbor, being honorable no matter your circumstance. Your circumstance is your circumstance. It's your encumbrance. It's what we do in the midst of that encumbrance that always matters in the light of all eternity. And all of you have that: a willingness, a nobleness, a strength, and Spirit, and fortitude you didn't even know you had.

And how often have you heard stories of the supernatural within the human being that suddenly without a thought, in the midst of terrible disaster, people do superhuman acts. Do you think they could have ever done those acts if they had thought about it in a rational mind? They never would have. So the thought wasn't even there not to participate. They participated not from the human but from the Spirit. And it's the Spirit, the God within us, that delivered the supernatural power. That's how close it is in us; that's how powerful we really are. We had a window of opportunity to exude our magnificence.

And how many times have you given in trust to someone and they couldn't give you back? How often have you held it as a grudge? How many times did you simply just forgive it? Oh, I know, I know the rational mind that says, "But this, this, this, this and this," but the God says, "What is this in the light of all eternity?" How many times, as has Yeshua ben Joseph begged us, he says quite beautifully, "And forgive us this day of our debts as we forgive those who are indebted to us." Isn't he calling upon the holy power of the holy Spirit to influence us this day, that by these acts we are no longer disingenuous but that we are genuine, to a true spiritual power that on the Plane of Bliss is simply this way?

And yet on the other side of that, have you taken and, through the light of forgiveness in one rarefied moment, given it all back? Because it wasn't demanded of you; it arose in you. Isn't that beautiful? You all have these qualities. How many moments have the innocents prostituted themselves in front of you and that the grievous nature of the human being has been there to malign and take advantage of — it's so easy to take advantage of ignorance and innocence — how many times in one moment do you arise to your greater spiritual self and walk away? Many of you have done that, to where it seems in the human monkey mind that "Here is an opportunity now to get what I want from someone." And how many of you walked away and allowed innocence to be innocence without corrupting it to your own advantage? You have all done that, not continuously, but you have done it. That's how we are. That's how we really are. That is how the structure of the self is. That's to your credit.

And have you — when put into a position to where the moment was explosive and that there was a feeding frenzy going on — that in that moment elected not to be explosive and rose above the clatter and the clanging of high-pitched voices and defining boundaries and rose up and became your truth in that one splendid moment to where there was no such thing as right and wrong, and that you rose up and shone what a true spiritual, noble lord is all about, knowing full well that if in one moment you thought about it, you might make enemies? And knowing that if you thought about it, you might be rejected; you may not be invited back; they may not like you anymore. But something greater shone through you. That is this essence. And you made a memorable mark that you will never ever have to have stripped from you but that adds to what you really are.

How many opportunities are you placed in, to where the living truth of the Spirit is able to speak instead of the cunning of the flesh? Why, you're in them every day. How many opportunities is it for you to shine what you are nobly when it would be easier to hide and to become pale and run away?

You've all done this. And this is your beauty. This you will never have to be ashamed of in the light of all eternity. And it is not something that you have to own in this lifetime; it is the fabric of the construction of self. And you all have that to your credit. It takes a truly remarkable man and woman to be in the fire of social consciousness and suddenly, in a blinding moment, know the right path and to take it.

Resolution is sort of taking then those splendid moments to your credit and applying them in the areas that you're encumbered in and not to apply it with human logic because it will always have an ulterior motive, as you know, but to apply it forthrightly from that which is termed the spiritual self that created it somewhere else.

I tell you it is a finer thing to walk away from the emotions that rip and tear you apart. It is a finer being who can get up off of their knees and dust themselves off and walk away. And they may have nothing when they do, but they are finer, more ennobled, and more spiritual in that moment than in the fray of who's right and who's wrong. It takes a very powerful person to do that, but those are the acts that give us this defining quality of God.

You chose the spiritual learning. That's why you're here. I set up the format. You chose to be here to learn about that which is not completely tangible. You learned in this life to help to define you instead of living in the fog of life after life which, on that plane before you were incarnated, all of you here found a central core of something that needed to be done. You needed to study. You needed to define what it was that has been forgotten instead of going over those same meaningless experiences and never finding resolution to them. So you chose in heaven a part of your linear process and, if you hadn't, you wouldn't be here. There are no victims in this audience to the spiritual teaching. It is here by design and by choice. You are following your soul's journey. And what higher life could anyone live than to live the life that defines God because ultimately that's what everything is. And you chose to be here in this learning because you obviously thought that I knew what I would be talking about, and so it was important enough for you to tarry with me for a time and dedicate a part of your life to gaining this. In that potential you created, you saw its value, of course, and you remembered the different road I took rather than the one you have taken ever since. You remembered that.

And so you're here then to be dedicated to the knowledge that I'm giving you and to teach you how to think, not as a fractured God but one that is whole, and to keep showing you through processes, though very difficult, can be very simple. And you chose to be here.

The spiritual godhead is the resolution to everything because it is in it (the spiritual godhead), that when we learn about self, then self is no longer cloaked in mystery. Although it's much bigger and broader than any painting that we could put forth, we still begin to have a sense of its presence. We begin to study our tracks and we begin to look at the tracks that we've made. And when we do, we will be closing in on the invisible presence that has made them, and you're here to know that. And when we do, we will find all of the answers that resolve the encumbrances that you are all dealing with. You have heavy ones that you obviously haven't been able to get out of and so you have gone to the fountainhead itself on this plane to find your way out of them and be free of them.

So how do we resolve? Resolution is so simple it can happen in a moment. It's the same moment of clarity that happens when you finally give up your past on the field and you lay that focus in clear water and then it happens. It is a dynamic showing you that all we must do then is to be able to move above our past and no longer affiliate with it. We must do the work as the human to forgive in every quarter that we can find forgiveness, because only then are we forgiven. It must come from ourself. To do it out here gives permission for the God, or the prodigal son, to come home and the tears of joy are passing through that emotional barrier. At every area in our life we must look to see what bothers us, what infringes upon our peace, what drives us and who drives us, and why we keep thinking in terms of the past rather than the present. And we must get rid of it by taking our energy off of it. When we do, we become whole.

That is not to say that the drama of tangible reality doesn't continue to play; it does for a while. This then brings into full *forebearance* the teaching of looking at the table and seeing it filled, even though it appears to the eye to be empty. Forgive, forgive, forgive, forgive; release, release, release, release; allow, allow, allow, allow. At every act of the way we become empowered. Remember, we want it all back. And it's locked up in the past. We want it all back.

Now here's the frightful moment of doing that. When we do that, we sometimes cut the lifeline to our own sovereignty, don't we? In other words, our sovereignty, our boundaries, our definition of love and companionship are all based in these places we're about to cut out from under us. We are literally pulling the rug out from under our carnal life, aren't we? Well, that's what the spiritual journey is about. We want to do that. We want to take the box and shake it up and throw it out there because only until we do that, yes, we are going to fall on our face. Yes, everything ceases for a while. Yes, it is going to happen. What else do you expect? "Well, the cupboard's empty but I'm empowered." Yes, yes, you are. But if you ever dare to regret that the cupboard is empty, you're not empowered because isn't regret also an empowerment of the godhead? Isn't it? You have to stop regretting. There cannot be any regrets, none, because if you do, you're fractured. And what we want is not to save face but to become empowered again. Understand?

Now that makes us naked and vulnerable, it seems. And we get the shakes and we are nervous. But if we can hold that pure place — it's the same place that finally happens when you break down and finally tell the truth to that fool. You know, you don't even care any longer what the repercussions are. It can't be any worse than what you've been experiencing. Have you had those circumstances? And when it's finally done, you feel so light, don't you? You don't care if the house falls down around you. You feel light. That's spiritual. That's the Spirit. Well, the Spirit then is starting to float. It's coming together again. And that's where the training on how to start applying pure power to what you're doing starts to become so important.

Now when we have resolution and we get to work on this in our life, how is the best way to work at it? Well, you have to stay conscious, you know. Now you can work eight hours of the day unconscious, but let's dedicate at least two hours of the day being conscious, being so conscious and so aware that we really influence the other eight hours that we really do make an impact, that in those conscious moments I train you how to first release the energy from the first three seals, which is the grounding place.

It's the first discipline you ever learn to do, to pull that up. I teach you the discipline and it's proved by science that it works. I teach you to do that. So first you have to get out of this plane and you have to be able to become mobile in the Spirit, so you've got to take the energy out of these places (lower seals) and they've got to come up here (7th seal), and that's what C&E does. And then if they're up here, you can shoot on into the Void, and you should go there. You should allow yourself to dissolve into nothing. I teach you how to move to points of light, how to become mobile, and how to turn around and how to be literally in the Void itself. Remember, consciousness and energy are creating reality. This is our natural place, in Bliss. We are imagination.

It's our product. So we have to go home to our natural self, our productivity of imagination, and that the Void is where we dip into to be cleansed, to be purified, to be free of our attachment.

And then when we're ready, when we're unattached, then we can move from the Void back into Point Zero again. Then we move from nothing into God, from nothing to God, and that at God we're at the pinnacle of our spiritual self. How long does this take? It is dependent upon the master. Some of you for an hour of blowing, you still won't get there; others of you, two breaths, you're there. There is no standard. It's all individual. It all means how deep are you ingrained in the first three seals and do you want to get out of them. Some people don't like to get out of them. Some people want to feel tired in the mornings and they want to feel this and they want to feel that, so wherever their want is is where they are.

So the closer we are in working spiritual, that that becomes our prerequisite, then we want to wash ourself of this body and we want to go and take a swim in nothing and then come back to the godhead absolutely pure. We're at the spiritual head. We are now in the observer's point of view. We are getting now to take a look as we start to fall from Point Zero, and we fall into the fifth, fourth, and third levels, which is what we're going to do when we start imagining. We're going to come back to a very familiar place. This is the place where we created the opportunities in this life from and we're going to fall into them. They're going to become very familiar. We're going to fall into those and, as the observer, we're going to allow the review of this life and what we want to accomplish to pass before. The line of potential has already been set up for you to do. It's easy to do. So what do you want to work on? You want to become unencumbered by your regret.

Then what is going to happen are all of the people, places, things, times, and events that regret is attached to will start to pass in front of you and, each one of them, you do the same thing with. You address it; you are now consciously addressing it.

Or it may be forgiveness. Remember I told you you can tell who you've run into from the Plane of Bliss, who you've made a deal with, is going to be the most difficult person to forgive, and that's someone that agreed to play that part for both you and for themself. And you're going to have to root it out and you're going to find them and you're going to have to address it. And when it comes to your parents, a most precarious relationship, you can no longer sit as judge over another person's actions. And so far in being the victim, you have been their tormentor. You can no longer sit in that place of power to hold them responsible and blame them for everything in your life. You're going to have to set them free because only in doing that do you get the power back that is no longer rooted in blame. Then you're free. My God, you're free. And you can feel it as it starts to wash you.

And you may spend the next six months doing that same process until one day it's a no thing. You'll wake up in the morning, you'll look out that window, and it's not there anymore. God be it that we are so empowered. The moment that we decide to do this is when we start the true spiritual path because it means that we are reaching for a higher and loftier order to refrain the lower order of ourself. Do you understand?

Do you see the value of taking thus what you have learned here by choice? Remember that; that's empowering to you. You came here by choice to learn this by choice, so you already had a head start, as it were. Do you see then the value of addressing the retrieval of your power, and can you see clearly that attitudes, all based in the past, are where the power is locked up? And how many of you see the value of applying the discipline on a conscious level daily? Can you see the value and what it will bring as far as ripening fruit in your life? Do you understand that?

Now that's the means. That's how we're going to get it accomplished. The sticky part is we can take care of superfluous things that really are deep in our core. But we've got to reach down and find those issues that we talked about when I said to you when you face now the fracturing of your God and heal it now, there will be nothing to look at in the light to come. And with that we begin to see more that self becomes more identifiable.

It's really a God that once it is freed up from its encumbrances, its burdens, of finishing up its creations, look what is standing in front of it that has an enormous wealth and revenue of reality to bring forth. And because it's not cluttered, it brings it forth quickly, not in a long period of wait.

The only reason you haven't gotten everything that you want is because you have too many things standing in the way of it. What you want is future; what stands in the way is the past. How could you possibly make room for the future when you don't have any because it's cluttered by the past? Simply wanting it isn't enough. There has to be power to instigate it, power to imagine. How can you possibly imagine an unimaginable when your thoughts are always riveted to some little emotional trauma that you're feeling? You're not going to imagine the unimaginable if you're thinking about food. You're not going to imagine the unimaginable if you're sitting there suffering, if you're sitting there regretting, if you're sitting there wishing you could be somewhere else. There's no room for it. There's no God for that to happen, so it won't work. That's why it's important that we do this by sheer choice because then we give ourself enough power to follow through with what we're learning, don't we? You never ever have follow through if you don't want to be here. Runners don't come; nothing happens. You have to be open for it. In resolution we become clear of our past, and it's no longer there and we don't have energy on it. The master hunts it down and digs it out and roots it out and confronts it, confronts it for the sake of self.

It's really incidental what anyone else does. If you have made the move to retrieve your energy back, if you forgive them of something they can't quite let go of, then the rubber band bounces back in their face, doesn't it? And the energy of it comes back to you. Then it's their issues. It has nothing to do with you anymore. And the way you'll know that, that no matter how much they try, they won't arouse a response because there's nothing there to arouse. It's as if the incident never happened. Do you understand?

Now this makes for sort of an interesting day, doesn't it, when we continue to have resolution. And it should be your focus, because what are we going to talk about then? What do we have to talk about? It's sort of the same thing about what do you bring to the table to a master. Why do you think that you deserve to be in their presence? You don't, anymore than what do you have to talk about if you've resolved the past with someone, someplace, something, some event. What do you have to talk about? There is nothing to talk about, is there? Are you understanding what I'm saying here? That's when you know you're free of it. You don't have to have an appointment to go back and to rehash it. And sometimes people just like to dig up the past because it takes them out of the present backwards, because they think they have to do that. There's nothing to talk about, is there? That's when you know it's finished.

Why *languor* there anymore? Why would a master want to sit there and talk about you to you? Why should they want to do that? Well, it's the same analogy. Isn't that what we want to be? Then why do we want or have the need to go back and have a conversation if the conversation was always based upon the dynamics of regret, resentment, failure, heartbreak, loss. And we could put that in all kinds of categories: jealousy, envy, betrayal, all of that. If we've resolved that in ourself, there's nothing to talk about, is there? So what kind of conversation are you going to have? Are you going to try to regurgitate it and get it back up there and start working it back up in a frenzy so that you have an equal playing field?

And this is what then becomes — as you're going to start to see very clearly — what is called enlightenment. You begin to see why you have grinding relationships: They grind on you; things that grind on you. You know why? Because it's over with and the only meeting ground that you have is to meet on those conditions. You don't know when to leave. You're a little confused on obligation here. You don't know when to give it up because the only thing it's giving you is this friction back here. You've grown. You don't fit anymore. That's when you walk away because that part has been played and it should be finished.

Now what does that do? Is your human intelligence going to tell me that that means you just kick your friends out? They're not a friend; they're a God. You have no beholding to any God but giving them freedom. That's the way it is.

True friendship doesn't grind. It grows together. It's Gods growing in ultimate freedom together. There is no grind there. That's why I tell you there is no lack in it. So when are you going to go back, go back for the sake and keep rehashing it because that's the only premise that you can meet equally upon? Tell me, my beloved people, is that resolution? No, that's regeneration of fracturing; that's what that is.

We must walk away. We have nothing to talk about. Think about the basis of your conversations every day. What are they based on? It depends upon the person, doesn't it, the place, the thing, the event. It depends upon that, doesn't it? Well, why revisit it? It's over with.

Now there's grace in that. Isn't it grace to have a community of individuals as family, but that in that greater spiritual family there is no dominion and there is no *agreeance* in that family to meet on the conditions of any past, and that the family are each individual Gods, that there are a forest of them that are growing? And that as the energy grows and changes in one, it's spread to everyone else. That's what we want.

You're confused about friendship. We made friends in paradise. We made friends only because they became closely associated with us in our journey here in integral parts and we've met them along the way all through our lives. And we've yet to meet many more who just wait for their part they're going to play in the potential that is yet to be unfolded, when the self has been healed. And they're yet to come too.

In God we are one. We don't have to make that clear delineation. When you helped your neighbor, you didn't think whether they were your friend or not. You helped them because it was something urgent in you that did it. That's the sort of relationship I'm talking about. Do you understand?

So be it.

IV.
Heaven

So here we are now in that wonderful place in paradise, in the Plane of Bliss or Heaven, however you wish to talk about it, when, as our true self unencumbered, we were plotting and planning on how to get on with this business down here and to heal it up and to make decent folk of ourself. And along the line we also had the privilege of going to great halls of greater learning. We were able to watch real advanced beings at their play and marveled at them. We got to walk into great halls of knowledge to where the mind of God is bound up in however you desire to see it, whether it's masters, it's books, clear revelations, dancing holograms. We all got that. You all got that. And you got to see what you were capable of asking to see. You understand?

So there was a second part to the Plane of Bliss that said, "Now if I can become unencumbered, what then is my real journey then once I'm free?"

Freedom. Then we have got to set about weaving that. What a marvelous and exciting opportunity that is because, again let me remind you, in the true nature of ourself we got to see it immediately. And immediately we planned a linear line that is really multidimensional because it takes in the entire triad for the distribution downwards to this plane (Earth plane).

And if we've arrived here and we have become unencumbered and we took care of the unfinished business, no matter how long it takes, then what begins to happen, and what you should understand is — now this is where thinking interdimensional, when I gave you the teaching on dimensional mind, this is what I was endeavoring to show to you — that it appears to be that things happen in a linear flow but in reality they are enfolded into something we've already created in a different time up here, a much more rapid time. We created for ourselves a great and marvelous adventure.

The masters know this because as soon as they're free that one fine morning, this all kicks in and they know it. So they're clear. Their mind is clear. They have no shadows. They are pristine. And when they do, then the deeper analogical mind gets to unfold the picture of potentials.

Now this is how it starts to appear. Phenomenon, as society studies it, is mystifying because it acts as if it is independent of all the laws of physics and indeed all the laws of energy conservation. And do you know why we'll always be mystified? Because they're trying to place linear phenomenon that happens dimensionally, and it's not going to work and they have to have a new caliber of science to address it. That is the reason why, when teaching you basically and simply about quantum mechanics, I gave you an understanding of a true science that, although it is only a branch of the tree, closest defines the way that reality behaves. And who is really in charge of that reality? Well, we created using, if you will, that physics, a dynamic adventure on the other side of unfinished business, that for the most part you never got to experience or even got to see with human eyes.

And so what begins to happen that baffles the conservative individual on this plane is that phenomenon seems to appear in spite of their laws. Well, where is it coming from? Who is the real guide in your life? Why do things fall into your lap? And where is true inspiration coming from? Is it really the law of randomness? Or is it more closely akin to a divine law? And the divine law is always imaging and imagination. It happened on a stellar plane of existence that now is being able to be brought through here.

What you're going to start to see as you approach clarity is that some very obvious signs are going to happen: A long period of not knowing what to talk about. Well, maybe that's the true silence, eh? There's nothing to talk about so you have to be silent. And then in that, because we are not regenerating the past and we're no longer fractured or we're working on mending up the temple of self, then we're becoming powerful and clear. That means we're spiritual. We are spiritual. We are our original self rather than our lower self.

So what happens is suddenly we start to see apparitions. Suddenly we start to dream lucidly. Or suddenly we seem to be very busy going out of our bodies at night, and it seems as if it just came onto us. Well, nothing just comes onto us. We've resolved something to make room for our great future plan that we have laid out in Bliss. And the phenomenon that starts falling in our lap is coming from heaven. And we are the Gods that are dropping it right on us. We set the plan up; we set the siege up. It is not happening by accident; it belongs to us.

And so we start inspiring the mind with thoughts. And there is no guide. There are not guides that are independent of us. In other words, we didn't elect somebody to take care of us while we were down here. We don't need to do that. We did that. We are our guide. And so what begins to happen is that we start to appear to us down here. We as observer and as subjective participant let out this program. And we're intricately involved in it. And where we make room for it, it starts to appear. And it is we who are appearing to us in our radiant body.

We start taking hold of the body. The soul has kicked in now. The pages are yet to be written on the great adventure that has been mapped out in heaven. And so phenomenon starts to happen in our life. We start to see lights dancing around our faces in front of us or dancing on some inanimate object. We also start to see things moving. It's as if we could see shadow people to the sides of us. We are becoming lucid. We have set this up. Suddenly something that we didn't even know we had the capacity for doing, we suddenly have a talent for. Where did it come from? It came from Bliss. Suddenly we know how to do something. We have the urge to be something, and the opportunities just fall like magic into our lap. There's nothing to curtail them from being there. And then the jolliness is that we get involved in a new aspect and a new adventure. Things start happening to us. They don't happen to us at random; they were put there by us. And the long dry periods where nothing happens are only because we're still fractured. The moment we heal, we're clear and it begins to emerge.

And what also brings this about is foreknowledge. Well, the spiritual path prepares us for our greater work.

Now there are students who in the dialogue[5] days would say, "What is my destiny?" I'm going to give them their destiny in a matter of moments. They're never happy with my destiny progress,

---

[5] Dialogue is the term given to the events held prior to 1985 in which Ramtha taught to small audiences on a one-to-one basis.

my report on what they should be. Their destiny is to clean up their act so that their great destiny can be unfolded. And they will say, "Well, what is that?" And I will say to them, "Unlimited knowingness." Now how could I tell them anything else? How could I say to them when you've cleaned up your act then something marvelous is going to happen to you and it's going to be this, this, this, and this. That would never have worked. Do you understand? It doesn't work that way. Your destiny is to be a God, not a woman or a man; a God, and in the body to be able to implement the extraordinary. The extraordinary will fall into place in front of you; and then you experience it. You'll move through it very quickly and always with a state of bliss because it was created in Bliss, don't you know? Hardship is created down here in unfinished business and through the friction of holding on too long. That's anguish; those are the hard things to get rid of. The potential that lies in front of us is not. But what does this mean? It means that when it comes upon us, we've mapped how to get out of our bodies already. We've mapped astral travel because it's the next great frontier. We have mapped meeting other beings. And why? Because we have so far lived in a very isolated form of existence to where in our *altered* ego thinking that we were utterly alone, we also went a step further by isolating ourself and our own turbulence, our past.

How can other life forms be a part of our past? And if we continue to live it that way, they will never be there. We are going to have the opportunity to be able to communicate with extraordinary beings. I am not talking about channeling nor am I talking about hearing a little voice in the head. I am talking about contact where we have now come out of our solitude and our prison into the open that we've already worked in because it is superconsciousness. Superconsciousness is the union of all-God. And when we walk in that union of all-God, then we're going to be exposed to that which we never could have been exposed to before. We are going to meet incredible people that seem to appear out of nowhere. They've never appeared in your life because they weren't scheduled to come in until resolution. Do you understand that? And it will only come when resolution is met.

There are extraordinary beings. How do you know they are? Because you've already met them in Bliss. When you have contact with other life forms, you've already met before and it will seem very familiar. And your first thing is you're going to say, "Well, we've had. . . we shared a past life. . ." Wrong. Get out of here. Don't even try to tell them that. No, we have met in the plane of God and this is just a reunion. That's what it is. And why did you have them there? Because they're part of the adventure. Just like you've had entities who have been part of your healing, that you met that are in this life, there are also entities outside of this life that live in other places that are part of your meeting to open up your knowledge and your awareness. Do you understand? And they too need those moments to meet because it's on their agenda as well. You're never taken at random. You're never engaged at random. There is a purpose behind it all.

And on the other side of that, what other things happen? Well, just the fact that you're whole and can maintain that wholeness without the temptation of falling backwards allows a time of rejuvenation in the body. You're going to get to experience true rejuvenation because it too is a part of superconsciousness. And then if all of these marvels are about to happen — true love, true devotion, true nobility, the true stewardship of a great spiritual mind — if all of this is going to happen, imagine the bounty that awaits us. Well, that's why so few of us ever come back because what is to come back for? What is to rehash for? Now this is where those celebrated masters are right now and they are in the extraordinary adventure and they have stairways to other dimensions that they climb in and out of with ease. And why? Because they seated themself on the throne in their bodies instead of their *altered* ego. And because their identity is to their spiritual then, they are connected with the mind of God which is whole. Imagine the access they have to dimensional life. It's extraordinary. You're going to have that as well.

Now why did I teach you to do the list? And what was the sacred teaching of the list? The sacred teaching of the list was to push cognitive buttons, to press them daily into your life so that those cognitive buttons are only aligned with what is going to happen from here onward.

And when we did that list daily and righteously and focused on it, we were catapulted back to somehow a place of reverie, of familiarity; that as we did that list, there's something in it that was acceptable. It was familiar. It was true. These are the elements that I am. Because in order to do it righteously, you must become an *imaginating* Spirit. And as long as you can hold that, then you are in your godhead because that's where you belong.

The list [6] was created with sacred dynamics in it to push the buttons of what lies on the other side of resolution and to push them so much in this life it would give you a reason to go forward, because all that I have given you is simply what you have already laid out. That's all. The list then follows to usher in the adventure. And you all deserve it. It's basically, "What can I do to be *deservant* of it?" Take your energy back. Do not be encumbered.

And there are layers to this, you know, that underneath doing it, there lies guilt. Well, guilt has to be addressed, doesn't it? And then when you remove guilt, then the responsibility is there; it's layered. But we are here to do exactly that and to move onto that so that we have the kingdom of heaven.

And when I tell you that to just get the idea that you're going to live for two hundred years starts the process, it starts the engines up of a concept that already lives on another plane. When we can accept it here, it makes our resolution easier here.

Let's pause this moment and reflect. Given where you are now, this station in your life, can you see that if there weren't certain points along the way that you finally resolved yourself with and walked away from, given where you are at now, who would you have missed? Look at who's in your life. What opportunity would you have missed? Do you understand what I'm saying? If you would have stayed where you were before you started this journey, what would you have missed out on so far? Who

---

[6] The list is a daily discipline taught in Ramtha's School of Enlightenment and used by the student to create reality. The list is a list of affirmations spoken in the "I am."

in your life, right this moment, would you give up to go backwards?

This is my point. My point is that on the other side of this, what is so intently your journey, lie great and marvelous things that you'll look back and you'll say, "I did the right thing." You always do the right thing. Sometimes in the middle of it the emotions get in the way or the humanity gets in the way, and of course in there are the layers of attitudes that are so empowered by God that we are fractured into that get in the way of the marvelous. You have not lived the best part of your life yet. That is yet to be lived.

Now common people whose journey isn't this, they're going to find peak points in their life where they peaked out. You know, they were at the point to where they were at their greatest in youth. That's when they felt the friskiest. Or they were at the greatest to where they were a prepared mind academically, or they were great in climbing the ladder to success and they finally got on top, or they were achievers and they finally created something that was the pinnacle of their achievement, or they finally got the person they always wanted or the child they always wanted. And you know that moment is their peak. And they're locked up in that because no one has told them that there is more. They think that once they have reached that pinnacle of success, that's the way it will always be. But it always fades after that.

You see, there's nothing like the luster of the height of the experience. But soon the experience, if not allowed closure, becomes an irritant and you grow old in its shadow and you long for its days. The common people without true spiritual training think this way, and we have seen that consciousness and energy does create reality in this school. There's no refuting that. So without knowledge, what is the best hope for their life? To say that they achieved certain things in their life and to be able to have to live off of that for the rest of their days, they only go down hill from that. Because, you see, that peak moment will never come again. It's done for. And that's all they wanted because they don't know to ask for more. And to ask for more denotes from this society a very greedy attitude, but that's the way that it is.

Now I want you to know, they don't have anything else to

look forward to because they don't have the knowledge to understand. And they're going to have to die, go to the light, look at this life, and go back to the contemplative garden of the commoner. And they're going to have to try to figure out a way to get themselves jolted out of this. And one fine day or one fine moment it will occur to them that perhaps the whole problem here is what really is myself. And when they ask that question, then they'll come again into this life and this will be their journey, to be able to define that. And when they do, they'll have those answers and then there never will be a peak; it's just climbing that ladder into eternity.

That's what I'm here to teach you. Everything that I have told you is. And it's only *conjecturous* to the point that you apply your lack to it, everything I've told you. When I tell you that the moment can cease from here on out and you'll never grow old again, isn't that consistent with consciousness and energy creating reality? But there must come a unity of consciousness and energy powerful enough to hold that moment forever. Of course there is, and it's not going to happen with a cripple, a cripple who has devastated their temple for the sake of holding phantoms of the past. It's never going to happen.

And doesn't it make sense that if you address your inequities here, they will not have to be addressed somewhere else? You see, everyone is headed towards the light on a freight train. That locomotive is going on down that track, headed for that tunnel. They're all headed for it because they need something different in their life and that's what it's going to be. Death is a reprieve from the boredom of a life of one who peaked out in earlier years. It just is.

I also tell you this and I'm telling you that it is possible to never die. It is possible to ascend this body. We now understand how that is a tenable, workable, and simple concept. In fact it is the natural concept because it is what we are on Bliss. And when we make heaven on earth a righteous place, which is our job to do, we don't ever have to die and we don't have to put this pitiful little body in the ground and let it be degenerated. We have the power for restoration, to restore it. And we have the power.

When someone says, "That is a very powerful person," did you ever stop and think what they're saying? Well, you may denote that in saying that, they're very confident; they have a lot of faith. Absolutely. Total confidence is the ability to have imagination and know it irrefutably, no matter what is going on around you. That is pure power and it makes everything else look so small.

What is a powerful person? A person who is unfractured. And what do we call them? They have faith or they have a strong will or they believe in what they're doing. It's the way that we endeavor to analyze what they have that we don't have. They get the job done. Well, why is it they get it done and you don't?

And you'll say, "Because they're powerful." But is that an unequal comparison to you? It's to point out to you that you don't have it. But you do; you just placed it in unfertile ground. Powerful people have magnetic personalities because they are deep and rich in imagination and that faith is unshakable in them. That's why you can't change their mind. That is a powerful being and that is what you need to be. And you need to be powerful in addressing and knowing. "I know that I am going to live forever. I know I am my radiant body," and it is unshakable. And when you have that kind of power, your list will be incorporated immediately into your life because that's the power that brings it into manifestation: unshakable, unyielding, undeniable faith.

That is a powerful person. They cannot be swayed by anything to take them off of that center. No matter what you show them, no matter what you reason with them, that person is God. That's a God that you're dealing with there. And you can say, "Well, it's idiocy. I can show them how they're wrong." Only you know it's wrong; they don't know that. Who's going to win?

That's Bliss alive and well here.

Everything I've taught you is. It is refreshing because it's an opportunity to have a life that hasn't even begun to hit its high points, that a new standard of life has been set in your life spiritually and that's where it needs to be set. It's going to make it a lot easier to get rid of guilt, its nonsense, and a lack of self-confidence. We have a lack of self-confidence because we're not empowered in the area of confidence. When there's no power, there is lack. Understand that. There's no reason to feel that any longer.

And as a side note, we were meant to be together. And you in this time in your life were meant to be right where you are and you're moving and steaming ahead. Not everyone in this school or reading these words will be able to retain the total message because the *altered* ego is very strong, and the coward in the human is very strong not to address issues of self that need to be addressed and cleansed because they're afraid of what they're going to find. And ultimately the ultimate message will never be received because the coward in us is afraid of confrontation, not of anyone else but of ourself and our secrets.

Not everyone in this room or reading these words is going to attain the walk of a master because most people are going to spend the rest of their life cleaning up after themself only to create a mess again. Why is that? The spiritual matter hasn't mattered enough; that's why. And when we labor to put God back on the throne — and ourself instead of our humanity — when we do accomplish that, everything I've talked about is ours. But when we still insist upon identifying ourself with past archetypes, past behaviors, when we insist upon violence as a means to an end, we insist upon brutality as a way of making a point — I understand all of that — when we don't want to give that up, when we insist upon business as usual, we don't deserve what is on the other side. That's why it's always safe. That's why some people are never going to make it because they can't change.

Let's celebrate today the good tidings of your choice. The good tidings that though in the moment it may not seem profound and effective, it's going to be. Let us celebrate that we're alive and that we met again. And let us celebrate all those others that are falling into our life from our future and let us make room for them. Let us close the door on the past and free up all the phantoms and ghosts and tormentors that only existed in our own mind. Let us close the door on that and walk no longer in the land of the dead and walk in the moment of light and freedom here and present, always present. And you don't need to find a reason to rehash yesterday or to blame. Let us rejoice. And the good tidings are that we have found through our efforts collectively the ways and means in which to address that.

I have never asked you to give up your virtue. On the contrary, it is what makes you beautiful. I've only asked you to change what needs to be finished in your life so that something greater can be made room for. Let's celebrate that we have made an effort to make that possible. And by no means should we close any doors on those possibilities. Let's celebrate that in a moment we can be God and that we have a life and that we are here on the place that it needs to be worked out, that it can be worked out. And if that becomes our agenda, then we're on line for the Plane of Bliss down here. We're getting the message and it's working.

So be it.

My people have joined us. They have been here since this afternoon. They are only slightly above the great hall. And for those of you who had that ringing in your ear today, that's because they're there. And that's not an accident. They are the grand and marvelous workers on this plane and they have done many extraordinary things. They are very interested in what is being taught here. And not because they don't know that; they do.

You must remember in my time before my birth, these were the great elders of this plane, you know? They were the holy beings who kept track of the galaxies beyond the north star and that's where they came from. And so they had a life that was quite different than the *Atlatians*[7] They were, in your terms, to be considered very holy people, brilliant people but very holy people. They were, in contrast to the *Atlatians*, profoundly spiritual.

And also the great north is important to them because on these

[7] Atlatians is the term Ramtha uses in referring to the people of Atlantis.

shores, the very ground that you stand on today, was once the beach land of that great continent and so here the energy is magnificent. The energy that was once their homeland, we stand on it today.

So I want you to know they are here. They are listening. They are observing reactions. And it isn't so much that this is groundbreaking knowledge, but perhaps it's the first time that a group has really listened to the knowledge and perhaps followed it openly.

One day it is inevitable that such beings as these that sit above this great hall will be able to finally show their presence to you because you will have an understanding, you will have some background and knowledge, you will understand that they're not about worshipping and they're not about clinging onto and they're not here to save. They are your brothers. Perhaps you could say they are your very evolved brothers. And watching your evolution is like great parents who watch from afar their children's growth in kindergarten. So they are very interested in how you're reacting and if, for example, in the light of the chaos of your lives, it makes a difference. This is what is important to them.

I am happy they are here.

V.
Walk of the Master

O my beloved God,
purify me.
Bring unto me
the activity of my holy Spirit.
Bring me up
to sit upon the mount
of my glorious being,
and direct my life
according to my wishes.
O my beloved God,
love I you greatly.
So be it.

To life.

Do you get a more enriched and yet more personal sense of those burdens in your life, what your job really is to do now? That's your destiny, to do that so we can make room for the extraordinary to happen in your life, and the extraordinary will happen in your life. Just as in those rarefied moments of analogical mind a little wonderment or a little miracle could creep in, there's a lot more where they come from; it's making room for them.

Now at this particular segment, we are going to talk about then how are we to live if we are then to switch posts. If what we are here to study to be, spiritual beings, then we have to begin to associate ourselves in that context rather than in the man/woman/biophysical context. And that's very important.

In other words, we are endeavoring to switch roles with our God. We want to take that place, that important post, in our life and to begin the work as if we still lived upon the Plane of Bliss, as if we were still occupying heaven. We want to be that entity. That is an immortal, eternal being.

If consciousness and energy and free will are ours to create reality, then what is the loftiest identity that indeed you can create for yourself? To simply say, "I wish to be and desire to be the God that I am, the entity who lives in Bliss and that is my spiritual self. My spiritual self has a reality all its own. Where is the nature of my natural homeland, for it has certainly become more obvious that this isn't it." This is the homeland of the physical. The spiritual homeland is in a different place.

So when you say, "Where I really come from, what my thoughts are, are immediately transacted into form instantaneously. So close am I to my energy field that my consciousness and energy immediately react," obviously in such a place then there certainly wouldn't be room for backward human thinking, would there? There certainly wouldn't be a place on the Plane of Bliss for jealousy and envy and anger and all those that lead to war. War is here. So we couldn't possibly have those kinds of attitudes and exist in Bliss.

Imagine how devastating if every thought that you had as a

human being over the last six months, if it manifested instantaneously, would you even be here? No. There are some real safeguards to evolution, aren't there? There are some real reasons why there's only so high of a plane that you can exist upon to where you have such a radical form as this, because you can't go back to that place and be all the things that you think that you are and that you are so righteous to defend here. When you are endeavored to be corrected, or it is pointed out to you that you are victimizing your life, it angers you because you don't want to hear that when it is pointed out to you that you're greedy or you're selfish or that you have very definite boundaries and that you're a survivalist and that you're clever and that you're manipulating and that you are a user and that you are an abuser and that you are a hypocrite. You don't even like to hear that, but the truth is you are. And in endeavoring to correct that in you, well, it isn't going to work. So herein then you'll get to lie in the spoils of that which you keep and hold onto.

The spiritual self isn't like that at all. And in Bliss there is nothing of that because in Bliss there is only the Spirit and here we have the body. So then we have to learn that to construct the God that we are is to construct the self, and we have to pay particular close attention to the detail of reconstructing the holy self. And that we understand that if we choose to be that, that holy place, that our energy is going to manifest it. Now to do that in the body is the spiritual work and the walk of the master.

This is where the master truly takes form because the master is mastering the difference between the human and the God, the Spirit. The master's calling is to be this because he understands or she understands that to be anything else is to be an unempowered human and they make that selection up here, very clear and very distinctive. And once they do, they go about their life conquering themselves. And the conquest of self — as we have already discussed in depth — is taking back the power. And what it means is it's not just running up to someone and saying, "I'm taking my power back from you." That isn't what it is. It is extinguishing the elements of attitude that we generate: greed and avarice, jealousy and envy and war, manipulation and hypocrisy and dishonesty. That's where the heart of the holy Spirit is fractured to. That's where the divine self is fractured into.

So the conquest of ourself is to take back our power from our own human self. Once we do this and we make a clear distinction, then that should be the first thing that goes on the list. And the new list should start with:

> This day I am my holy, holy divine Spirit.
> This day I will create from the mouth of
> that holy Spirit the following things:

And we work on being that, and we make the mantra so that it is repeatable during the day, that it can be drawn upon as a place to raise back up to because during the day we're going to have the propensity to fall back into that which is termed the animal self or the human self. If we can carry this throughout the day and continue to say it throughout the day, we keep reinforcing and bringing ourself back up the elevator to this holy place. And there we do our work from.

It's not that you have to change jobs; it's just you have to change beingness. And you work from that place as the holy Spirit, understanding that most human declarations of self and all these things that we have discussed don't exist there, and the appetite to go back to them must be curbed through that primary holy self. We are rebuilding the holy temple and it is inside of us, and there we are rebuilding ourself. And those attitudes cannot be fostered inside this temple. They are unholy things. Do you understand?

Now what I just told you is not hard to do; it just takes in a moment a passionate desire to choose to do that, just like you chose to come here. "I choose to do this. And I choose to live this way rather than the other way. I choose that. No one has forced me to do this. I am not doing it out of guilt or remorse and I'm certainly not running away from my human. If anything, I am taking a stand against my human." And that's very simple to do. It doesn't have to have a lot of ceremony to it. It only has to have passion and intent. When that's there, everything will start to follow.

And then everything that comes to you during the day you're going to address from the temple, the holy self, as a God instead of as a personality. And when you address it as a God, you will administer your day righteously, knowing all day long that everything is God and what you do to someone else you have done to yourself. And the idea here is to bring the power back inside of us.

Now that fundamentally will start your first day off rather wonderfully. You can see subtle differences in everything. You'll begin to see that in the morning when you fall into a slump or a depression, that when you simply move the basis of your consciousness back to this place and contain it, we'll find that there is a refreshing feeling that starts to come over the body. And you won't have the propensity to fall into depression or into fatigue. You'll be able to hold it.

And the longer you'll be able to hold it, sweet and wonderful things start happening. The little things of the future start creeping into your life. They start falling in front of you. Hard edges become softened. The hard and narrow way is abolished. There seems to be a growing of presence. Well, that growing power of presence isn't anyone standing out here; it's you radiating from in here outward. It's radiation. Understand?

Things respond to that radiation. Life responds to that radiation. Everything responds to it because it's life-giving. The holy Spirit is life-giving. Consciousness and energy are life-giving. And when we are at the highest point of our being, the plant life that is around us responds to us. It won't be uncommon for flowers to bloom in our presence. It won't be uncommon for birds to gather above our heads. It won't be uncommon for things to begin to become enlightened around us. Animate and inanimate objects begin to shine a little more. That's because they are in a holy presence.

And what is the holy presence? I tell you, people, it is making the choice to be God and executing your life from that window, from that temple, and from that place. And the radiance is life-giving. To hold something in your hands, immediately that something or that person or that thing will be rejuvenated. And it's not that you hold them to be rejuvenated or to rejuvenate them; it is a natural product of radiation. It is a natural product of a very high field radiating. You understand? And all it is is taking the platform of consciously being that definable self and every point of the way taking back the power, slowly taking back the power. Nothing gets to you, nothing, because if it does you get fractured. It's the way it works. You'll see the results immediately.

Now this is the actual placing of the one foot in front of the other, the walk of the master starting to walk now and along the way conquering the past and unencumbering, unencumbering, conquering, gathering more power. And the more that you do that and the more you unencumber yourself on a daily basis, the more intense the radioactive field becomes. And it is radioactive except it is not radioactive in a *deformative* measure but rather a restorative measure because it is coming from a holy place.

And it's one foot in front of the other. It's moment by moment. It is living from this place. I promise you that if you can live one day without transgressing to your past, you will not have known time that day. If you can live two days without returning to your past in any way, in any thought, in any action, in any deed, and you can hold the presence of the holy Spirit, you have lived in the moments of eternity. You will not age; you will radiate. Understand? And the field becomes permeable.

Then the question arises, as it's going to with very physical people in here, "Well, what do I do with my body?" Well, you're stuck with it. What do you mean what do you do with it? It's yours.

"Well, what does it mean to take care of myself?" Well, which self are we talking about? The number one reason you're here is to take care and rebuild self. That's the spiritual path. If you were here to rebuild your bodies, you would be in the wrong place at this point. We're here to focus only on the core of creation, including the body itself that hangs on the Spirit and is worn by the Spirit.

How do we then take care of this? Well, if we move to a place of God and we are reconciling and rebuilding our holy temple, then we have to understand that the body is the garment of the temple and that the radiation is going to come out of this body.

Furthermore, the body has an emotional body that all of our power that we have placed extraneous to ourself is going to come back to us and will pass through the barrier of that emotional body and will be felt in the garment, to be purified and to be brought back to this perfect place. And then every time we call it back, it's going to cause the body to weep. It's going to cause the body to be depressed. You're going to feel emotional when you call your sons and daughters of energy back home because they pass through the gate to get to the inner sanctum. And it's passing through this gate that they are purified and made clean. That's how we get our energy back.

We don't want our energy to come back to us and be lodged in our soul as jealousy. We don't want jealousy back now, do we? All we have understood now in the teaching is that energy then wound up is in a conscious form. It has an agenda. Well, that energy is our God energy and that if we have misplaced it and if we have placed it in an area that brings us to our knees, that defines even the noblest of our sweet and indelible character, that when we call it back it has to come straight back to us as jealousy. And it's going to penetrate the emotional body from which it was sent. Do you understand that? And it is going to come through and it will come through the body. It will react on the body first and reverse-fire all the way to the brain. And you're going to feel it. But only until it does that then is it relaxed energy once again that then can come home as power to the temple within. We have to have it back.

So we must have the body then as a fortress, so to speak. And that the holy temple is inside the fortress. And this means then that we have to purify what we have put out because the only reason that we are here with our dreams from Bliss is because it is only here that we have to rectify and render complete our unfinished business. That feeling, to feel it into action, is important in order for it to be identifiable to this plane of existence, for it to be a reality for us to experience. So now we have to call them all home.

The body then should be regarded as a garment that is going to be a dirty fortress for a while. And that every time this energy comes back to us, when we call back our power and it passes through the barriers, when it gets on this side of deliverance, the body will be burnished a little brighter and a little brighter and a little brighter.

So how should we think? Well, we really aren't our bodies, but they are the fortress to which we inhabit to do the work here. And if God is living in this fortress, then we should keep the fortress clean and make it a holy place. If we, however, think that the fortress is us, then we have fooled ourself back into using the body to find our own pleasure. We're not supposed to do that in the spiritual path. Our pleasure is in the kingdom called Bliss in which we create instantaneously.

When we get up in the morning, then the next statement on this list is:

> God bless my body and burnish bright
> this day my holy temple and the power of my
> marvelous works. This day uplift and heal my
> beautiful body.

We do that, then we have included the body.

To what extent should we go then to be physical? This is going to be a gray area because we've been this so long that to be the holy Spirit and then to go up and eat our way through several pantries of food, there is a little falling, if you will, of consciousness now.

We should not look at the body as the resource for pleasure. That's very important. When we stop seeing the body as the *necessitater* to pleasure and that the Spirit is the only one that is, then there's some wonderful things that happen. The body's appetite normalizes. It may find that you don't have a propensity to eat all the time because you're being nourished on another level. You understand that? And that you should feed the body when you have the hunger and feed it and give it to it.

Should you then be radical about health? Well, health begins in a righteous attitude because without that, even the healthiest entities die of heart attacks early in their lives. Health should not be an issue. What should be an issue is a healthy Spirit, a Spirit not crippled or not damaged or not broken or not splintered but contained, because when we do that — remember the teaching I told you about that the body is the last kingdom to which all of our thoughts manifest? Well, so it is that we could look at injuries in the body, deficiencies in the body, and we could look at disease in the body as the final resting place of our splintered personalities acting from the *altered* ego place.

We certainly have created in this world of technology a great deal of Band-Aids to put on it and a great deal of medicines to heal them, but you know they're only temporal. They're not going to stop time. And time, as we have learned today, is the eroding of the past onto the present, and the body is going to fall. Its energy cannot be sustained because every time that we support our victimization, every time that we point a finger to someone and blame them for our life, and every time we complain then about our life, even though it is seemingly serving us in the present, that body is going to take on that law. And take it on, it will.

So the health of the body really is not about the nutrient factor; it is about the spiritual factor. If health was all about nutrients, then God is taking second place to vitamins. Do you understand? We should be very clear on this. Now just think about this for a moment, about where you have coagulated discomfort in your body. Think about where you hurt, where you ache, what your propensities are: You eat too much or you don't eat enough, or you think about eating all day long. Where is consciousness? It's about food intake. It's about exercise; it's about this; it's about being buff; it's about fat; it's about all of that. That is not a master. There is a great hypocrisy at work here.

What we need to do in taking back the fracturing of that, which is termed our God, is that every time we call that home to us and it passes through that emotional barrier, it's also passing through the very aspects of the body that became degenerative because of its original passage.

So then the body maps perfectly our reality. It shows you all of our weak points. It shows you all of our lecherous points. It shows you our decadence. It shows you our worries, our fears. It's all lodged emotionally in the body and it's degrading it. The button is pushed on.

When we then in the morning sit about proclaiming that we

are the holy Spirit and that we elect this day to live as a pure spiritual being from a place of power, when we do that and we start eliminating our encumbrances and finishing them and that energy comes home, the energy will also be drawn out of the knees and the back, the ears, the nose, the eyes, the reproductive area, the feet, the bunions. It will be drawn and sucked right out of it because if there no longer is this need to keep propped up the reality of our past, then we totally, through a spiritual place, pull the energy out of these places that are the reason for ill health. And it goes back to the Spirit. It's purified.

And what does it feel like when it's coming out? Well, it's sort of like that thing that I told you about, that process you go through physically. You'll feel those very areas ache. I want you to know it means that the energy is being pulled out of them. There's like an octopus that is being pulled back out. Because as we own our past, so we own it utterly and totally, including the body. Those places will ache. They will bear fever and, when it is done, they will radiate with health. Now that is health.

If you elect not to proceed in this because you're a coward, you're not ready to look at your life and you're not ready to forgive and you're not ready to forget because there's so much of your day-to-day experience wrapped up in that victimization, and if you're a coward, and you're not going to look, take vitamins. Exercise heartily. Keep it up for a while because otherwise the nutrients aren't going to get there. The unfortunate thing is that the vitamins and exercise do not postpone aging and death. They are inevitable because that's the law. It's how it works.

But the care of self should be a clean radiating Spirit that's so pure and uncorruptible and that that place that holds its place radiates true power; that is health. And the body will start to conform itself like a God. Remember we're lawgivers. The body isn't bigger than us. It's when we are too cowardly to be its ideal and we put upon it our miseries and complaints and small-mindedness.

So the body should be cared for but it should be cared for

---

[8] Refers to one of the side effects of practicing the C&E breath technique in the beginning to where protein floods the bloodstream and causes - in common terms - a cold, where you are dripping from every orifice to where your acid body is changed into a protein body.

from a place of understanding that this is going to be your vehicle.

This is the body that if you are a true adept, this is the body you will ascend in. So what do you need to change? A lot, and it's all attitude. All attitude. And when the attitude is changed, the healing will occur. Self-pity is a crutch. Excuses, "Well, I'm not really ready to give up chocolate." No one has asked you to give it up. "I'm not really ready to give up this or I'll not give up that." But those things are connected to some attitude up here. I am not asking you to give up anything except your humanity and be utterly spiritual, because you're going to see that the radiating power of that energy restores.

And, you know, when you're not fractured anymore, the eyes start to heal and you can see again. When you see clearly in Spirit, you'll see clearly in eye. And when you give up that fracturedness of that fear of insecurity, you'll start to hear again like you've never heard before. This is the power of the alchemy to which we change from base to Spirit, and it's easy. All we have to do is, "I choose to do it and I'm going to execute it." Do you understand?

So then the question arises, "Well, should I or shouldn't I?" What you should be is spiritual, the core of God taking its power back. And you should also understand that the body is a molding and it's really designed to be molded around attitude and it's designed to house attitude. So one clear test is that if you couldn't hold up under an arduous day of walking or marching in the field, then you need to change some attitudes. You're too much the body and not enough power of the Spirit.

Exercise is marching. You get up in the morning and you take a brisk walk in a foggy morning outside and you inhale the air and you go deep into the forest and you come back. That's a march. It's also spiritually rejuvenating because it is being in touch with nature. And if we are to start our day as natural beings, then do that. If you find that appalling, then start your day as spiritual beings in your bed. You understand?

You know, your body should never have been the excuse to not do the work. And, if anything, you should have changed some attitudes to make it so that it could do the work here because, remember, this is your choice to be here. Your choice is to be a spiritual person. You've given your power away to food. You live for it. You think about it. You've given your power away to lethargy; you'd rather do nothing than do anything. You've given your power away to your body.

Or you're the opposite. You've given your power away to your body so much that you're not a spiritual person, but you look good. No one's home, but the house looks good. In some arenas that would work very well but not this one because we're not trying to be an image here any longer. We are endeavoring to be what we are in that blissful and beautiful state because that really is our natural state, and that to suggest that you're looking good to wear a piece of cloth, if to suggest that a piece of cloth makes you look better, well, that is such a foolish thing. We wear the cloth and adorn ourselves with silk and satin or roughly woven wool, whatever it is that we want, but it does not change the station to what we are. We can be brilliantly beautiful in rags, equally brilliantly beautiful in long silken robes because what is really the beauty is not the garment. My God, that's going to get old fast.

When we become that spiritual being, we are going to be after energy; we really are. We're after it; we're going to bring it back home. And the more that we get filled with it, the more we're going to become. So that field of radiant energy is naturally going to come out of us and we will have more energy to do more things than we ever dreamed about. We will get tired less and we'll be able to hold that dramatic fulfillment of the extraordinary much longer. And if we're not encumbered by the past and we're not burdened by it, then we are really free. We're like great steeds that have just broken loose from the wagon. We're free. We can run and run and run and run. Do you understand that?

Moving energy from the first three seals to the fourth center, the holy place, increases metabolism, because it's a movement up of energy. And, more important, when we drive energy to the brain, we are affecting critical seals in the brain that are attached to, as you have learned, glands that are the key centers for turning on hormones. And those hormones that turn on in the body do a cascade all the way down.

Now if we don't drive energy up there, then those centers, those glands, start to slowly close down. And pretty soon all we're living on then is the glands that are around the first three centers. That's what we're living off of, because really that's what it comes down to. That's what the personality is based on. That's its food source, the first three seals.

When we become spiritual, we move it and we start activating the brain and we're activating the fourth center. We are literally starting a raging fire inside of our chest, inside of our head. And the energy, once there, and brought back over and over and over to rebuild and to redefine the self, radiates enormous power. Well, that energy is what turns on the hormones of perpetual youth. When we start activating the brain and the fourth center, we increase everything in the body; it's a natural flow.

Cleanliness. If you know that you are approaching the altar of the holiest of holies, how would you come? How would you stand before Christ? Filthy? Covered in the perspiration of the poisons that have been exuded from your body? Is that how you would stand? I tell you, great saints never did that because they understood what the baptism in holy water was really about. It was washing away the crusts so that the perfume or the musk of the Spirit could permeate the air.

Don't be confused over this when I talk about the musk of a man. You think that is your perspiration? Perspiration is poison. It's noxious. That's why it has such a terrible odor. And those noxious fumes are poison. If you continue to live in them, then you are inhaling them back into your body. Doesn't that make logic to you?

Well, they're being excreted for a reason. If your body wanted them, they would have kept them. Do you understand? It would have kept its smelly business to itself. It's trying to throw it off. When I talk to you about the musk of a great man and a great woman, there is a smell that accompanies the Spirit when it's in-house, and that's its musk. Its energy has a fragrance to it; the fragrance is a thousand flowers in bloom. It is the highest melodies put to smell. It is a symphony of all creation put into scent. The Spirit has a musk. All great beings have a musk to them and the musk is the radiation of their energy. Just like the body radiates from it, it's cleansing the toxins out of it; the Spirit also radiates, but its radiation smells like heaven. And to be touched by a master and then to continue to smell that touch, that is musk. That's what I am referring to.

And when we clean the body, we clean it and we oil it and we perfume it. We are inviting the spiritual musk because it's pleasant; it's beautiful. The Spirit is not that which we would not want to be in its presence. It fills us completely sensually. When you stand before Christ, you be clean in every orifice. You be clean in every crag and every pit, in every curve, in every fold. You be clean so that to stand in the presence of greatness is to uplift your own greatness and to allow your own musk and your own permeance to come, and it will come.

The less we are human and the more that we are spiritual, the body is going to change. The less we are concerned about that which is termed the body's dynamics and what it eats and what it doesn't eat, and the more that we place our focus in being that spiritual being, we're going to change the dynamics of energy in the body. That is the natural flow.

And we want to change them because we want to be what we really are, a great and magnificent self, undefinable but definable, that great and magnificent being of consciousness and energy that bares the soul of remembered experiences that broadened the parameters of its existence. That's what we want to be. And when we live through spiritual energy, then we generate a radiating field that will be a field of musk.

You should always bathe your body; seek cleansing as a true cleansing. The toxins that you wash off of your body, the day that you start this process, are the residue of the chemical changes happening in your body. Wash them off; clean them off. Don't keep inhaling them back into your body; clean them off.

When we start to make this dynamic change, the body is going to go through many shifts. Clean it, polish it, oil it, and get ready then to meet the holy Spirit again in the night or in the morning, and make your commitment to be that. And you come to it pure. Don't come to it tattered and dirty. I don't care what you wear; that's not going to conceal the toxins. I'm concerned about where the temple is built. You come to that place pure, and then we receive the holy Spirit with clean hands, oiled and fragrant. You'll notice a difference. There's no excuse not to. That's why God created rivers and streams. Take a dip.

Now when we begin our day, whatever job that we are laboring at, we are laboring there under a fair pence, salary, wage. Now it is honorable to fulfill and to execute your duties for which you are being paid. There is no master that ever walked that did not do this. And some of them worked very menial jobs. It was an excellent way to observe their attitudes. When you take the throne of the holy Spirit — and number three on your list is:

> Let me execute my labors this day
> from the just place of my holy Spirit.

The question is then, is it suddenly because you've become spiritual do you deserve a raise? No. Raising spiritual energy is the raise. That isn't even questionable any longer. It's not about getting the shekel for the effort; it's all about the effort. And that's what we're interested in.

If we are now sitting at the place of power, in a place of spiritualism, then what we're really interested in is our interactions. That's where it really counts.

We want to be able to put the holy Spirit into a magical place, and the workplace is a magical place. It isn't an excuse to fall back into old habit patterns. It's the ideal place in which to start taking back power. It's not taking the power from someone else. It's taking back the power that we've placed there. That's what we want to do.

And when we then work for the honor of our Spirit instead of for the dollar at the end of the day, we are now laboring in the fields of God, and that's where we should be because on the list further down is going to be this question of fabulous wealth.

Because the closer you become spiritually and the more consistent you are, the greater that reality is going to become.

And you're certainly not going to get fabulous wealth on the job. It's coming from the Plane of Bliss. And it's coming in a wonderful extraordinary door that opens up to a whole new adventure, the adventure that we all, at least most of us, carefully planned out. And that's where it's coming from. It will not come from your job.

But then every day our idea is to execute our duties righteously and deliberately and without cutting corners because, when we do, then we only cut our corners. Do you understand? In other words, we don't ever cheat anybody but ourself. And if you can tolerate that, then I have very little respect for you. And if you can cheat someone else — and you're cheating yourself because that's where it comes from — I have very little respect for your humanity and for the power of your Spirit because you have been placed in a place of trust by someone who was willing to pay you for that.

If we decide to become spiritual people, then we must no longer look at the application of our life in terms of dollars and cents. It really needs to stop. We should rather then search for the application of our Spirit in day-to-day ways in which we empower our Spirit, because that's where the great mother lode is going to come from. Do you understand that? And to slough back off and to move into an attitude of cutting corners and taking too much time and too many liberties, yes, you are cheating your labor, but the worst that you're cheating is yourself. And the worst is you think you're getting away with it. That's the lie. You never will be because what we do, we do to ourselves. Have you gotten that point yet?

If we move then from the first three seals of the survivor — we've got to get a job and we've got to pay this and we've got to have that and we've got to have this and we've got to have food on the table and I can be nice until we talk about money and I draw the line — that's the first three seals. That's the animal that I referred to. When we move from that place, we really move from that place and we move here (4th seal).

We're rebuilding the temple; that's what we're after.

Our God is always going to provide for us because as long as we are endeavoring to become that spiritual and righteous being, that radiating energy field that I said that will be noticeable the first day, that radiating energy field, the more that it is empowered, the more powerful common thought becomes. And just imagine, if you will for a moment, our natural way to think, that if we have common thought issuing from the throne of our God, from this high place that we're going to sit in now, and we have common thought coming from that, then how close are we then to that reality? We are making it fall out of the heavens. We are closer to home. We are closer to our true nature than if we're down here.

The spiritual journey then should not be about dollars and cents. It should be about spiritual growth. That is not to say, however, that you should sit on your haunches and let someone else take care of you because, you see, in that you also betray yourself and you harm yourself. You harm yourself in ways of not having a place to go during the day to where it challenges all facets of your being. You need a place of challenge. You need a place to where you can apply this in the workplace. So it is getting up and going about your business and executing them and discharging those duties righteously. Because at the end of the day, you're going to know if you did it or not. And if you cut it, you're going to be cut. Do you understand how this is working?

And the same way with being the lord of the job. When you have to give permission for the entities to do their creative work, and you hired them to execute creative work, stop running over them. Let them be creative. Allow them room to learn in your presence. This is both ways. And a righteous lord is very rare. A righteous and fair and loving lord is very rare. When we all have the responsibility of people in our hands for eight hours out of their day, we'd better be a righteous lawgiver because what we do to them, we do to ourself. And if we abuse them and if we make them seem small because their duties seem so insignificant to the larger picture of our own life, we are the fool. We are the one who is really small.

Every laborer who gives to us eight hours a day or nine hours a day of their life deserves respect and honor. And they should not be looked upon as servants, slaves, the old tendency of the hierarchy to be served by ne'er-do-wells. Although in the idea of the Spirit, a true spiritual being is one who is in service, isn't it?

When we remove all of these attitudes of higher and lower, then there is a radiating field of love, and we shine and we grow and we bloom in such a field. To abuse anyone in our trust, no amount of money gives us the right to do that, no amount of money. And if we cannot be compassionate and loving, yet *directful*, if we do not give these marvelous lives room to create, using our territory and our time in which to fulfill their duties but in a creative and challenging way, then we stifle them. Then we are stifled. If we abuse them and mistreat them, then we don't deserve them; we are not righteous lords. We have no need to be sitting in the power of anyone's place.

But if we learn to respect them because they are us and we them, when we learn to understand that they are God, as we are, and that we provide them an arena, a playground, in which to address the issues during their day, we have given them an opportunity as well as ourself. And when we manage them in a state of love, we will find that there really is no need for management, because righteous people do not need overseeing. Do you understand?

Now that is a loving environment where the garden can bloom, and bloom it will. And the weeds will not be able to take hold. They can be rooted out. A person who isn't a self-starter or a continuous motivator will become obvious. That's not the place for them.

So a great lord has the ingenious way of having ingenious people work and labor in their reality but give them room to create their own. And to do so in love and trust and in honor, how rare that entity is. It's working both ways, isn't it? We never do to someone what we wouldn't do to ourself; never going to do that.

If we know that within our boundaries there is a thief or there is a villain, we'll know it. We will know it because in Spirit nothing is hidden and it will be revealed. And the just execution of that is that it is also made known to the person who is the villain. And the worst punishment is to be exiled from a garden where everyone's blooming but you. That's enough punishment, isn't it? To lose the opportunity to really grow and be roses, to grow and be lilies and to be able to have the musk of spiritual creation, that is your just reward, not to be able to have such an environment. But of course you created it and you deserve it. It's not a problem of trust. When your lord that you serve sits on the throne of the Spirit, they're going to know everything because it is the natural order for them to do so.

So the job then should not be about nickels and dimes. It should be about applying an impeccable energy and impeccable thought processes.

Now those of you who bargain with each other, you have a very nasty habit in this audience of trying to take advantage of each other, and that should come to an end. In other words, if you ask a skilled craftsman, one of this great family, to make you something and they tell you how much it will cost, then that's fair enough. If you don't like what they charge, then you find someone else who will make it for what you're willing to pay. But don't try to bargain down these people from their labor. That is not righteous. It's not clever. And don't tell me it's in your heritage to do that, because that is a foolish and backwards statement. At this point there is no such thing as nationality. The Spirit is not a nationalist.

Y̶ou don't do that. You don't try to take away from your brother or your sister what they're asking for their energy. You ennoble them when you accept it. You honor them, don't you? You honor them and, because you do, if they are righteous, they're going to honor you in turn with superior work. On the other hand, don't you then take advantage of a situation that suddenly your fees last week were this and now, because it's this person, they have now doubled. That is taking advantage of. That is unrighteous.

We do not want to, in the spiritual life, foster — now listen to me — we do not want to continue to foster victimization, especially amongst this group. We don't want to be responsible for giving someone the opportunity to be a victim, not in this group. Do you understand? The game is off here. In this group we want to practice honor, we want to practice righteousness, and we want to practice trust. Don't set up the pattern by saying, "Well, they didn't like it so they're just being a victim." Don't you do that. This is a spiritual family here. Don't intentionally go out and try to victimize someone and then use the teachings to say, "Well, they're just a victim" to somehow justify yourself. That is in error. It is unrighteous and it is unspiritual.

We don't want to give anyone in this group even the slightest opportunity to become a victim, because this shouldn't be a group to where that is a choice any longer. Do you understand? That's a choice in the common world; it's not a choice here. And don't play the games out there in that world in here with one another. We do to another as we do to ourself, and what better group to practice that on.

Perhaps it would be refreshing to say, "I feel that you have undermined your price. I feel that this is worth much more than you've asked." Pay them for it. Wouldn't that be a shift? But isn't that then exercising the remarkable instead of the predictable? That's the little areas that we begin to nurture here. No one in this group should target anyone else in this group and victimize them intentionally and then make them feel wretched because they're a victim. That speaks very, very villainous of you, distasteful. And I know when you're doing it. What you do to them you're doing to yourself. I swear to you you are.

So in exchange, don't try to whittle down. Why don't you try the opposite? Why don't you appreciate? Why don't you find, rather than based on nickels and dimes, true value? Do you understand me?

Now have you gotten some clarity on this, what I have just talked about, about labor? You've got clarity on it, and what is important is that you have to approach that as a spiritual being and not as now then a physical being with a certain identity. Do you see the value in that? Because we're not just working for dollars any longer; we're working for freedom of the Spirit, and it is the most pristine place in which to apply it. And it works on both sides.

This brings us then to the money issue. There are those of you who wish and want for fabulous wealth but you bring nothing to the table in exchange of it. You're wanting unlimited wealth but you're the ones that bargain down people. You're the stingiest of them all. How do stinginess and unlimitedness become compatible? They are not. Let's go back to Bliss. Let's go back to that place in the contemplative area to where we are creating the lifeline potentials. Let's go back there now. It's not an issue on that plane but it is definitely an issue here, and the wise understand that.

In this life potential we don't bring wealth into the picture until we have taken care of our encumbrances. And maybe some of those encumbrances have everything to do with that; for example, the climb to the successful ladder necessitates that happening by the manipulation of gold. And that would be then included in the plan to resolve encumbrances. But we only bring in the alchemist's wealth once we have finished the program. And once it's finished, then we get to have it because it's clean then. It's clean energy.

And that then is a power that will open the door for some extraordinary events to happen here because it utterly and totally frees up that which is termed the physical from the need of survival and does not permit the Spirit to once again fall down in the first three seals to that old animal place of dog-eat-dog and the survivalists and boundaries and herdlike mentality.

But imagine this then. If on that place instantaneously we really have everything that we want, then it really didn't cost us anything to imagine that because that's our nature. Our nature is to have unlimited imaginative qualities. That's our personality, our nature; that's what we're supposed to do. And therein in heaven, or in the Plane of Bliss, wherever we elect to go or are capable of going, that measure then is delivered instantaneously. So what really is of value is not gold but the imaging quality of ourself, to be able to image it properly. So we have figured that in already into the continuation of the work. Every master that has lived longer or beyond the eighty-years of life expectancy, that has lived two more years longer, has already got the wealth.

Now here is my point. My point is that if we sit upon the throne of the spiritual self, then we can only be what we naturally are. We cleave to the imaging quality of consciousness and energy and there we must find reality, profound reality. It is how the Spirit is. The Spirit isn't limited by anything. It is only the consciousness of the body that limits and curtails us, and it's only because we give our power away to it does that limitation occur.

But let's look at this for a moment. How spiritual then is a person who wheels and deals? How spiritual is a person who will bargain you out of your last hundred dollars on a project you put in a lot of time? How spiritual is that person? They're not spiritual. That doesn't even make logic, you see, because the spiritual person coming from this place doesn't need to do that. You understand? Because the Spirit is never in lack. It is laboring to replace its energy, isn't it? It's not laboring to replace money. It's laboring to replace energy. And when you start cutting and figuring and finagling and trying to work someone down out of their price, you are, at that point, basically the most unspiritual you've ever been. You say that's good business? I say it's poor spiritualism. And who's going to outlive who?

And, furthermore, you'll never get fabulous wealth wheeling and dealing. It isn't in the program. It just isn't. It never will happen to you. I won't let it because it's not on this agenda. When it does come is when you righteously put into effort what I've taught you to do.

Fabulous wealth isn't going to come from cutting pennies and shaving someone's fee off the top just to save you a few more dollars in your pocket. Fabulous wealth is not going to come from that. It's going to come from those three stones in your pocket and that Spirit that's focused upon it in an unlimited fashion. It's not going to come from anyone else. It will come from the doors that open to allow it to happen. But to then become fixated on something is remiss. It's not how it works.

Now we begin to understand why many of you haven't received your fabulous wealth. You know why? You have brought nothing to the table to even show that this is what you are. And instead you are takers and not givers. There's a difference. The human is a taker; it's not a giver. It's the Spirit that gives. That's not going to happen. It just won't.

The actions that we generate from a loftier perspective is what's going to generate it and make it fall out of the sky or bring the extraordinary right to our door. We get to walk in the door. We get to always choose whatever we want.

And how much of your tangible physical assets are you willing to put on the line for your Spirit's imaging ability? Now that's walking it. We put everything on the line. I know an entity that has; everything. What does that mean? It means that the choice to be spiritual and to believe in the image of the imagination, that it is, is much more powerful and much more real than the assets thus accumulated that are in threat of being destroyed because of the dream.

When do we call it quits? When do we decide what is real, and is there anything that can ever break us? A truly spiritual person will never be brought under by tangible things. They'll never give up the dream, no matter if it means losing everything they've got. If losing everything they've got allows them to isolate the dream unencumbered, then so be it. How far are you willing to do that? There aren't too many of you in here that will do that because the energy has been placed in the protective *survivalistic* zone.

It's just like what we have referred to earlier. You know, you won't address your salvation because it means having to look at yourself and that's cowardly. You're cowards. You don't want to do that. Well, it's the same thing with this issue of being the Spirit. How much needs to be washed away before you break down and become human again, let it all go? That's a real test. That's laying it all on the line. And such an entity deserves the kingdom of heaven, wouldn't you say? That no matter what, they cannot lose that dream; they hold onto it. That is powerful spiritual reality at work, no matter what.

We're always safe in convention, as long as we don't touch this area here. We can play; we can espouse allegiance; we can espouse support; we can espouse that we're this or that until we're called upon to lay it on the table. Then we know what we're made out of. We really do.

It's no different than talking it up at the Prancin' Pony Inn about what a great warrior you are until the time comes to be on your mount at three in the morning armored, and drums starting to beat and bells starting to twinkle in the horse's mane, and you know you're going to a destiny and you're going to have to live it now. And are you really that big and bad and that awesome? It's quite a different tale on the battlefield. And it's sort of like the idea here, the idea that someone graduated from this school. Let's go, please, on the battlefield. Let's go to the field; let's have the test. Let's see if you're a graduate of the great work.

Coward.

You see, it's easy to talk and it's easy to proselytize. It's easy to say what you would do and wouldn't do, but you never know what you're made out of until you have to hold the dream and walk it. Now we know.

Is this God testing us? Well, in some quarters we would like to say, "You're being tested." No, just the act of holding onto an intangible while everything that is fundamentally tangible underneath you is being swept away by the tide of simply not having the energy there, that it is being swept away because all of your energy is going into a dream. Is that a test? No, it's not a test. But isn't it interesting that we would see it that way?

And why do we find that interesting? Why would I find that interesting for a person to say that? Because I know then that they have considered going backwards and recanting the dream. And to entertain that idea, they call that a test. It isn't. To a true master there is no other choice. There just isn't. That is not a test; that is steadfastness. You've got to stand in awe of a person of such power because they can't be bought off. They can't be threatened. Now that is an awesome being. We have people here that are going through that.

It's so easy to say, "I made a mistake." It's so easy to say, "I shouldn't dream such a lofty dream." That's easy. That's a coward's way out. It's so easy to say the day that we mount upon the heavy horse, "I don't feel well."

"Ride and throw up on your left. Every time those drums

beat, puke. You're going to ride."

You understand? It's easy to say, "I don't feel well." And, by God, we cannot feel well. Just the thought of it makes us queasy. Just the thought of losing all those things makes us nervous. Well, it is enough to make you sick. It's enough to make you sick going to battle. But then we know what you're made out of, don't we? And you do too. It's so easy to try to recant the Spirit. And so often it's done for the sake of convention, for the sake of good business, to justify our losses, to write them off.

It's also easier to say, "I made a mistake." We're absolutely willing to come forward in our brazenness and say, "I made a mistake" when it serves us to say it.

"Well, of course you did, good fellow."

"Whew. Got out of that one. And all I had to do is say I made a mistake; then everybody accepted me back."

"Good chap, good chap, good chap," over a deep draft of brew. "Ah, he was man enough to admit that he was wrong." Yeah, he was man enough. That's the only thing he was. Get the picture?

But he didn't have greatness. And greatness doesn't come from being a man or woman. It comes from the viability and the reliability of the Spirit that insisted upon seeing that table full no matter how empty everyone tells you it is. That is a spiritual being.

It's not a test. It's only a test when we falter, isn't it? Then it's a test. And it only becomes a mistake when we wish to recant our experience and get out of it and somehow paint the picture so that it's acceptable and palatable to our human consciousness that really wants to get on our case bad.

Well, you know, guilt is unacceptable to me and I never had it and I don't think you should either. And saying you were wrong is unacceptable to me. I didn't, and I don't think you should either. I didn't make excuses, and I don't think you should either. And that either we are made out of the stuff of the Spirit that rains down from the Plane of Bliss or the only thing we are is, in the final analysis, the assets of the faculty of our senses and our clever mind and ready victims, a ready storehouse of victims in which to prey upon for our sustenance daily, whatever that sustenance would be, whether it is dollars, affection, guilt, an exchange of power going back and forth, preying upon the emotionally weak, sexual gratification, no matter. Then that's all we have left and, I tell you, that's just not enough for me and it never was.

If you regret any of your past, you're still logged there. Isn't that so? When we leave no footprints of the past is when we have no regret. And how can that possibly be then? Because the past served us to finish the experience. That's what we're here to do, to make known the unknown.

How can we ever call an experience a mistake and have regret towards it? Who would we have been without that experience?

I can tell you we would be a lot less than what we are now, because sometimes it takes terrible experiences to bring us to our human knees so that our spiritual self can be born. And why would we think that is bad? We should be grateful.

Why should we regret that we had the parents that we have? And why should we regret the body that we have? Because to do so is to be locked into it and all the pain and suffering and misery that comes from it and that energy that's running out as the clock ticks, because we're stuck in the past. Why would you regret anything that has brought you here to this moment? Why regret any conquest, no matter how bad it smelled and no matter how bloody it was, if it brought us to paradise? Why would we regret that?

So a spiritual person who creates a dream and believes in the dream knows something. They know that that reality is alive and well in them. And if they can hold that reality in deference to this reality, that in the gaining back — listen to me — that all rejection that you get from the outside to your dream is purposeful.

And you know why it's purposeful? Because you can feed off of it. How does a spiritual person feed off of it? They transmute the focus into determined energy. It bolsters the dream somehow to a stalwart entity. And the more rejection, the more criticism, the louder the roar builds up around you, a true spiritual person will feed off of the energy and transform it. They feed off of it and that makes them more determined, and that determination one moment is going to break through because it's larger than life. It's mightier than life. How can we regret that? And why would we not want that? Why would we not want somebody to ridicule us?

Why would we not want that when we can feed from the energy, when we can take the energy and turn it into what we are even more stalwartly? Why would we want to do that? Why don't you see objection as an opportunity to enhance what you are instead of breaking you down? It's not meant to break you down unless you're weak enough to be broken down.

And I tell you greatness is that great and magnificent spire that is going to come off of that temple that is headed straight up above the heads of everyone. It's going to be noticeable that this entity is locked into a spiritual power. And the world could come and go but that power is going to be there. And the more we object to it, the bigger it gets. When it is strong enough, it will break through this plane and it will shatter everything. It will be a marching, raging army and nothing will stop its manifestation. I tell you, nothing.

Why don't we see criticism as food, building material? Why don't we see it that way? And why don't we understand that unless we hold the dream of the spiritual imaging self, we can't even then begin to be called spiritual, let alone a master. And if we have that certitude within us, then why do we have to come down here and monkey around in day-to-day- business cheating people, cutting corners, which usually means cutting ourself? We are really getting ourself cut out of the picture now, aren't we?

Money. It's locked into that fabulous future that was created on the Plane of Bliss already. But you have to go to the spiritual place of imaging in order to get it because it becomes very obvious that you have no faculty or asset large enough to create fabulous wealth, given your own use of your own brain and the little knowledge, much less the capacity. You don't have what it takes to generate that kind of wealth. The Spirit does.

So it's through then the kingdom of heaven that it arrives. So it is a gift of the Spirit. In other words, we gave it to ourself in another place. We looked after ourself in another place provided, of course, that we made this breakthrough taking care of unfinished business and resolution because it's dangerous to have that when you have an incomplete life, when you're in emotional pain and suffering, because it only complicates it. It doesn't make it easier.

You know, all the money in the world is not going to heal your victim life. Never has, never will. And all the money in the world is not going to give you freedom from your past. If anything, it's going to enhance it. So this is where we come then. When we have learned then to walk in the spiritual path on a day-to-day basis and executing and discharging our duties as a spiritual being, we are given the righteous freedom to hold dreams. That is the nature of the Spirit. And as we day by day take one step at a time in front of the other, the footprint that we left behind will dissolve and come back into us, and our radiating field gets greater. And every day our life improves. Every day our health improves. Every day we get younger instead of older. All of the good works that we do are mounting up, and we find every day then after a while that our common thoughts are no longer based in that which is termed the neocortex or the first three seals that are common thoughts that are rooted in the temple within.

We are beginning to think as Gods through imaging. And we have the power every day to be *enforceful* with those thoughts. Then our day-to-day performance suddenly no longer has a price tag on it. It is about then becoming God, which is everything, because when we have become that we have the power and the authority over all the riches and wealth. It is a no thing.

At the end of the day when we come home to our family, how should we come home? Should we come home burdened or should we create then the homecoming as yet another joyous experience? If we create the homecoming as a joyous experience and we have lived our day righteously, we will go home not tired and fatigued but elated, and we have many fine and wonderful moments to share with our partners, as they with us. And each gets their equal time in sharing.

So what do we do then as a spiritual person with people in our life? Where does sexuality fit into this? Well, to you this is as important an issue as money. But I tell you that when you are free of your decadence, you'll understand that sexual intercourse is really the representation of a union of God with self and its opposite struggling to be neutral, to be whole. And so it takes on a very sacred act. It's been humiliated, it's been destroyed, it's been debased in the marketplace, it has affected even the innocents. It is a sacred and holy act. And is there goodness or badness or right and wrong about it? No. There's only attitude.

If we remember that the body then becomes the temple of the living God, and if we choose to be that living God, then it is also up to us to choose who enters that temple. And it shouldn't be just because we are like the animal and we're in heat or the rut's on. That is a poor excuse. And everyone here except the children have experienced that sexual freedom.

And we've also understood then that there's something lost in it. There is something that doesn't complete itself in it. And yet if it is exercised and given in a state of pure spiritual love, then all of the seals open up and energy can make its run all the way down, which causes tremendous orgasmic feeling all the way back up to the brain, exploding into the head. It is the Kundalini experience in action.

But should it be something that is given casually? That's up to you. To a holy man or a woman, it never would be. It's not something that we casually do with friends; it is a sacred and honorable place.

Now we could have a great discussion about venereal diseases, and it doesn't take too spiritual of a person to begin to pinpoint where they're coming from, and they're coming from an excessive unsacred nature. They're disease, dis-ease. And if you have them, it's because you've exploited your nature. It's that simple. It is no other karmic thing out there. That is simply the way that it is.

And a chaste man and a chaste woman are the rarest things in the world. Chaste, meaning that it is sacred, it is holy, it is shared as a unified field. It is a field that is unifying between opposites, and there is one who has chosen to be that and it is shared. That is the most intimate of our nature. How much more intimate do we get than that? How much closer on the physical realm do we get to another person than through penetration? It's very close. The only other closest way is when we were in the womb of our mothers. That's how close and sacred it is.

The act is as sacred as a child in the womb. It shouldn't be anything other than two Gods coming together in a reunion; then it is beautiful. If it is used to barter with, if it is used like harlots, if you are a whoremonger, if you are a hetaera and you use it, you're going to die because you have missed the true beauty of the act itself.

When we are spiritual people we understand this and we understand the sacred value of the temple and we understand the sacred value of the semen and we understand the sacred value of the energy, not always going out but going up, right into the brain. We understand that. You have yet to understand that. And you use your sexuality — you have in the past as human beings — to get what you want, especially women. And they use it because men are weak to that area. All they know is they're supposed to impregnate the world, but that's the animal instinct that herds the cows in and copulates with all of them. They think it's their right. Only animals think that way.

It's been abused. And if you use this in abusing others, you're going to be abused. That area doesn't escape the immutable laws of this. What we do to others, we do to ourself.

Now there's no right and wrong, but there is a difference and a quality about engaging in lovemaking as a spiritual being rather than a carnal being. That's when energy is going to start hitting your head and doing wonderful things. Other than that, it won't happen. The orgasm only is orgasmic in the first three seals. It causes the heart to beat at an extraordinary rate. And that quickening of the heart doesn't necessarily mean that it's a good thing. There's many a good man and woman who have died in the midst of copulation because, you know, the energy isn't right. It's up to you. It's always been up to you. This is our temple. It's our place of sacred. It goes for every part of it, for every part of it.

Now you can disagree but you're only going to disagree from the human point of view. And you can say, "It is for us to experience and it is for us to lay with the entire world and that's the way it is." Then let that be your truth. I am telling you the way that it is.

Enjoy it. Treasure it. Love one another. Be kind and soft and considerate and compassionate and, above all, be God. Then we have pure magic at work here. After all, it's through the act that the fruit of the womb is born. It must be a holy practice and, alas, it is.

What about then the spiritual life in the roles of lovers? What should they do or didn't do? That becomes very self-explanatory, doesn't it, is that when we are fortunate enough to gravitate to this area here, we're going to have beings gravitate to us that are like us, whose energy sits in the same place, whose journey is the same journey. And then we're going to fall in love because, in that perfect union where there is no lack, there is no lack. There is nothing to create there; it's already been created. This is cosmic glue. This union is cosmic glue and it is beautiful. It is God-the-giver, and both are givers. And because both are givers, they are showered upon in receiving. That's sublime. Are there lovers that have been masters? Have been for hundreds of thousands of years. Are there other masters who don't have lovers? Have been for hundreds of thousands of years.

We want to love what we are. And if we are the dastardly human, spoiled and pricked by our past and weakened by the tragedies of our past, we immediately set about trying to change the person in front of us and manipulate them so they too can follow the same road back to our own path. That is a humiliating experience. But if both parties are used to doing that, then it's very workable. Both are victims and both suffer and they bawl away and suffer together. And they have, instead of one person, two people that can point the finger and that makes them feel really good. Human beings can have that sort of humanly love because it's a self-serving love.

A spiritual love is on a different order. It's not that at all. We don't want to have love in our life that's trapped in yesterday because that won't be love; it will be lack. We can't have the fabulous future in our present if we insist on breaking away to the past because every time we do, we leave that love behind. We leave it; it doesn't leave us because love is the constant.

When we find such entities — and you will find them — their relationship is one of healing and nurturing and you have an entity who doesn't point a finger, who doesn't regret, who doesn't make you responsible for making them happy, and you have created exactly what you are because these are all the elements that you are. That's why you are so beautiful together; you are so alike. Isn't it refreshing? Or could you even fathom that, having a lover who had no problems? Well, that then is truly a spiritual relationship because to the Spirit there aren't problems; there are only opportunities. Do you understand? Well, that's the way that it works.

And if you're sharing with many comrades and friends, you be wise about them. And you're only going to have gravitate to you what you are. And what isn't you, you should not spend time with them.

And old relationships that just grind, you know, they're always bickering, they're always demanding, they're always acquiescing, they play that game of tyrant/victim. "You did this, you didn't do that. Shame on you. You disappoint me. You hurt me" and all that garbage. You know, it once started out beautiful. It started out beautiful, intoxicating, clean, lots of sexual energy, lots of love, and you learned something from one another. You got an experience from one another. Perhaps that was one of those relationships planned in heaven, in Bliss, because they were key to sending you on your way. Now whether you get on your way or not is always a chance we take as spiritual beings when we inhabit the fleshy body. But they're there. They are supposed to be in our life.

The Plane of Bliss

But when are they not supposed to be in our life? When the learning is gone. When the learning is gone there is nothing but boredom. And what fills the vacuum of boredom? Arguments. You've got to pick on each other. You know why? Because you have nothing left in the relationship. You've got to somehow pass the time. You've got to justify being together so you pick on one another and you point fingers and you do all of this and all of that. It's over with.

We need to know when to walk away. And the sooner, the better, before it degenerates into such a complicated myriad of emotions that walking away is a confusing, haunting experience. And it's not that you still love the person; it's that you're haunted by the confusion. Do you want it? No. But what was it about? That's what haunts you. I'm telling you what it's about. You overstayed your experience.

Now a little side commentary about people who use the word 'love.' Most people who use that word do not know its meaning. So what they're really saying is that "I need you." But love often has been abused. Its terminology has certainly been abused by people to enslave and ensnare. And somehow when you tell someone that you love them, that means that they're supposed to let down their guard to you. That isn't what it is.

And so often when relationships are separated or broken or splintered — that term starts coming up a lot — it's usually by those who are wanting to hold on. And holding on does not justify the relationship. It's become a habit, a dependency if you will, a codependent relationship. It has nothing to do with love. It has everything to do with need and control. And just because someone says to you, "But I love you; how can this be?" Well, if it was absolutely sincere, it would never have to be. And because someone says that they love you does not mean that suddenly you should change the course of your life, to acquiesce love, because it's more of a habit and a need on their part to reinstate control, and it's used for that. The real and genuine article will come your way. And when it will, it will not be immersed in any of this game playing. And they won't have to be protective barriers and all of that and territories defined. It's a blending of the two into one. It's beautiful and it happens so naturally. You don't even have to work at it. It's already there and it's so sweet. That's the genuine article.

And it's not true that you have to work at relationships. Those that are made in heaven, you never have to labor at. Do you understand?

So be it.

VI.
Entertainment

Now where do we stand as spiritual beings on entertainment? Does the Spirit need to be entertained? Does the body need to be entertained? Always, always. Most entertainment today is not spiritually-oriented. The grand, grand symphonies of old were oriented to the Spirit. They inspired. The reason that angels are depicted playing harps, and why are they playing a harp, is because the music inspires us to the angelic realm. And that's really key. Those great masters who appear here, who have decided to be that in their outrageous potential, when they come here it is about playing the melodies of the celestial realm, of Bliss. And they carry it back here.

Now those true masters, very few of them are here today that know how to compose music to where the sound vibrates the brain into holographic patterns all its own. Just because music sounds good doesn't mean that it's doing anything. Do you understand? Because for the most part what sells today in entertainment is sex and violence and the murder of innocence, the rape of innocence. The violence sells. So that which is marketable and will always be marketable is what appeals to the lower nature of human beings. And rare is the audience that goes against the trend and can put a piece together that causes an upsurge of energy to happen somewhere else other than the first three seals. Those masters are long gone.

So at one time it was not that the Spirit needed entertaining but more like that the Spirit's heart needed to be strummed. And in those elder times, such great composers did the job. They knew how to restore the soul. They knew how to soothe the body and free the Spirit. They promoted, as it were, an individual path of dreaming in the celestial realm. That was natural. That wasn't entertainment. Today it's entertainment.

And it is so impoverished, I tell you. If you really know consciousness and energy create reality, then take a look at what is being produced in the marketplace. And what kind of reality is being cultivated? A collapse of the younger generation. They have no morals, no respect for life, none. And it is urged on by drugs. And when they are drugged out of their gourd, the veil is dropped and they are free to murder and maim and rob and rape and abuse, and this we call entertainment. The beauty of a woman and man is no longer sacred; it is a marketable commodity and either you have it or you don't. And what a cruel world we have delivered to ourselves and to our doorstep.

When we understand that entertainment is reality, then I would advise you, my beloved people, do not see what you're not willing to experience. If you're still fascinated by violence, if you're still fascinated by the degradation of the human body, if you're still fascinated by the perversion of sexual acts, you now have it at your disposal to be able to use and you're going to be drawn to it and you're gong to be entertained and mesmerized by it. It shows you where you're at. It's that simple; there is no hidden message in this. But when we sit entranced to that which is termed a play, is that any different than the one that we created on the Plane of Paradise? Didn't we create the play there to be players here? Then if we sit and watch someone else, this holographic potential being played before us, are we not then the participant and are we not setting it up in our life? Absolutely. What is proof of that? Commercialism. That commercialism will get you to buy something that you ordinarily wouldn't buy. Why do you think that entertainment is anything different? You're buying into the program. That's the way that it is. This is not to assert that you're not tough as nails and can't see anything unbruised; you're not that yet. You can be seduced right down into your first three seals and be locked there. And it doesn't take a particularly great-looking entity to do it. That's how susceptible you are. And you can be induced to rob from another person. It doesn't take a lot. All we have to do is have the opportunity. Because we've seen it, we'll do it. Do you understand? We're vulnerable, vulnerable. Entertainment should not appeal to what does not celebrate the Spirit in man and woman. That is not entertainment.

But be that as it may, you are free to choose to do anything, and I am not here to tell you you cannot. Because, ultimately, remember the law: Whatever you do, you do to yourself. You understand? So it's by your invitation. And many of the problems of your life can be pointed to entertainment, that you invited it into your life. But don't be a victim to it. You chose to be entertained. Do you understand? It's the way it works.

Alcohol

Now dropping the veil [9] through alcohol. You best be in a real clean place when you want that veil to drop down and you'd better make sure somebody's sitting on the throne, because the moment that you lose your faculty, in the first few moments the veil is going to drop down. And what environment are you sitting in? What's going to walk right in? A wise master knows this. A fool doesn't, or does and does not heed it. It reflects the wretchedness away and we're shielded in love. You should remember that.

I would tell you don't go and drop your veil in public places because in public places what we've yet to discuss are the levels of those people who didn't make it to Bliss. And where are they? In infrared.[10] And why are they still here? Because they still want what is here. So who are those people? Well, just imagine where they're hanging out. And if we then begin to understand that they are feeders and that they feed off of your experience because they can't interact in this world — you understand? They don't have the body to create reality so reality stops and all they do is haunt what live human element is working on here. They're going to hang out in those places. And they stayed here for a reason, because they were locked into a way of life.

If you could see what I see around your places of entertainment, you'd never go there because you're not ready to go there. You can go there when you're a full-blown master because you can see what's waiting on the archway before you get to the building. You can see who's on the building. You can see they're hanging from trees or on high lines. They're nudging in for the place, the best place, just like they did in life. And they're crowded. They're upon you like ticks fall out of the trees

---

[9] Dropping the veils is the term Ramtha uses that when one drinks alcohol, inhibitions are removed and thus one is vulnerable to thought forms.

[10] Infrared is the second band of frequency in the light spectrum which inhabits thought forms.

onto the deer's back, and sickening. They are wretched-looking creatures and they fall right on you as you move in. And they feed off of you when you drop that veil, and you will be caused to do acts that you would never have thought to do before but what invariably led to a shattering of one's own life. Because how can we blame them when it is us who invited them.

When we're a master we can walk up to such places and communicate with them. And when they know that someone really sees them, it's quite startling. Some of them run and hide. Some of them just stand pale in the face of awesome wisdom. Sometimes then they'll listen and sometimes they'll go on. Now that's what a master does. An ignorant person wouldn't even begin to imagine what is around them.

You have to be ready to see what you're going to see. Furthermore, you have to be ready to understand what you're inviting, what sort of lice, parasites, you're inviting on yourself. And, you know, I'm going to ask you: Are you really that far removed from being one yourself? There are some people who see this as a way of life. If it is seen as a way of life here, it will be a way of life after death. We've got to change it.

It is all right to drink wine. It is all right to drink hard drink, but just know that you're becoming vulnerable. And choose wisely the company to which to do it in. And never drink so much that you lose the faculty of reasoning because when you do, you've overdone it and you're killing your brain.

Drugs

Drugs on the other hand are made to emulate hallucinogenic stimulants or they are made or created to assemble themselves in such a way as to chemically distort neuron activity. They are the worst of all because they're the ones that destroy the brain. And in the case of marijuana, that weed was created to help suffering animals. It was called crazy weed, to go and find it and eat that would lift them out of their pain and allow their Spirit to move in a state of shock, which would then move the animal to water. It was a painkiller. But, you know, what is it that kills the pain? It's the dying of the brain, isn't it? If the brain is anesthetized, the pain won't be felt, will it? Well, it was created exactly for that by a very merciful group of Gods.

Now what you've done is you've used it to dull the sense of your own emotional pain and your boring life. But understand that the effect gives you a high, but the high is really the death of the neuron. It's the explosion of light and there's no recipient. The neuron is dying. It is created to do that. It's to numb the senses. It seems as if you have a heightened sense of awareness; you don't.

And it is no state to be spiritual in, because the last that we want to do is to damage the brain because it's the great computer in which we must use to finish our work. And if we damage any of its circuitry, then we are really working with a crippled piece of equipment that we've done the harm to ourself. And then I ask you what thing is too terrible to bear? Why do you have to get high? Because you're low down. Well, to get high means that you're low.

But what is wrong with processing energy? Don't you think you're strong enough to do it? True, the human being is an impatient critter. It's a nasty one too when it's cornered. But are you such a coward that you can't deal with the issues that you've created? After all, they'll never be greater than you because they came from you. Or is it that you can deal it out but you can't take it when it comes back. Really what a drug is is to numb the sensation of the return of what you meted out. I would think about that, if I were you.

Because why would you want to do that? Well, if it is for the sake of getting high and feeling free for a moment and if you can justify that those moments are worth the death of the brain, then it is your life, isn't it? But I am telling you how it will be reciprocated. You're a coward and you're weak, if you cannot deal with what you've meted out and deal with it. And if you have to escape your own reality, you don't deserve to be a spiritual person; you don't deserve to be a master because you don't have what it takes. A master does not run away from what it's created anymore than you would want to bail ship on going to work the following day. We have created this. It is our nature to be creators.

It is our nature to experience. There's nothing wrong with finding out what it is, but once is enough.

Drugs. Why do you need to justify them? Why do you try to make them into something that they're not? Do you need to excuse them? Is feeling good what is really so important to you? Well, what did you do today when I told you that when we start to address that which is termed our fractured self and we bring home our energy and we take it away, when we cut to pieces our past and we take our power back, I told you that it is going to pass through your emotional body. How are you going to handle that? Or does that terrify you? Do you think that if you get drunk or you get drugged that somehow that will numb the sensation of the prodigal child coming home? Why would you want to do that? It is only through that coming and that dark night of the soul [11] that the energy that we wish to take back can be purified. We don't want it to come back to us in the form of envy or jealousy or hatred or malice or cunning or avarice or greed. We don't want it to come back to us that way.

We want it clean so that we can use it to bring about a fantastic realism. So it's got to be purified. The only way that energy is purified is when it returns to sender. Perhaps this scares you, that you're going to have to go through a little suffering of what you put out. If you don't do it, you're a coward. And I tell you numbing yourself from its return is such a foolish thing because feeling good isn't what this life is about. It's about being a creator, not feeling good. You know, we don't create to feel good.

Now you can still do what you want to do. I have taught you well. I have reasoned it with you well. You're not wrong if you do and you're not right if you do; it's a choice. It's the same choice of becoming spiritual. It's a choice that we make for ourselves. There is no greater high than the high of God. There is no greater high than being spiritual, utterly and totally. Walking as Christ, that is the greatest high there is. And do you know you deserve to walk that when you have walked the path and bore it all. The significance of the cross and torment and suffering is

[11] Dark night of the soul is a state of depression that masters fall into when working to master self. The energy is coming back home through the emotional body. Also the master is awakening to the realization of the degradation of humanity.

that one is willing to go through that so one could be restored, and so it is.

We have to come to a very lofty decision in our lives before we can deserve the richness we've already created somewhere else what we righteously deserve. And if we can live one, two, three, splendid days as being that and only that, we won't have a lot to talk about as we have before because we can't pick up a conversation. We can't even say, "How are you?" Why would we want to say how are we? Why would we even want to ask them that question? Because that isn't even relevant to a spiritual person. Masters don't come up and say, "Hey, dude, how are you? Haven't seen you around in a while. What have you been up to?" They don't talk that way. God, only you talk that way. They don't say that.

So what are you going to do now? You're not going to ask them how are they because that's not a relevant question. It's not even a sincere one; it's just making conversation. And you should never tell people they look good because they've lost weight. That's a terrible thing to say to people. "Ah, you look great. You must have lost some weight." What does that have to do? That's out of the picture now; we can't use that any longer. The weight should not be a conversation of concern with masters; correct? So we're not going to say, "Is everything going well with you?" With the spiritual self it's always well. What else could it be? So what are we going to talk about? What a delightful day. Talk about an adventure. That is going to be one, isn't it? It will be so sweet.

If we can do that one or two or three days, my God, we're going to see the results of that radiant energy. We're going to understand when I tell you you discharge a field of radiant energy. You'll begin to see it. And you know you're going to feel better because you don't have worries and problems on you because you elect not to. You just elect not to. And so that means you're going to be lighter of countenance.

And another thing is that you're not going to be spending the day trying to be clever and ingenious and all of that, so that's not there. My God, how much energy are you going to have blasting around when you don't have to do all those things? A lot. Well, then I think you can take moles off of your body and, you know, heal your bunions. You'll have enough to do that then. And if you just follow this through for three days, you're going to see a difference.

It's enough for us never to have wanted to come back, isn't it? It's enough for a legion of us to have gotten a taste and grabbed hold of and never come back because there is something more to this, and I have only given you words. But if you've listened well, you have formed brilliantly those manifestations of language, of imagery, so you've thought along with me. You've actually imaged the teachings along with me, which will always be much more brilliant than my pitiful words are. But they're given to inspire those images.

So we've gone through then what do you do from the beginning to the end of the day. What do we say then when we lay our heads down on our pillow to sleep? We evoke our holy Spirit as self. We pledge our body into a safe place. We allow ourself to travel and to remember. And we set the art of casting a spell over our body while we are gone, that in our absence our body will be healed, it will be rejuvenated, and it will be filled with vitality when I return. We cast the spell and we go to sleep and, if we keep doing that, we will find ourself in vivid adventures, not in the dream world but in the spiritual world, the natural place to where we all reside.

And if we keep acknowledging the gratefulness of our life and if we keep acknowledging the gratefulness of our Spirit, then that becomes common thought and soon we start to think like that. We can then engage the rest of our list if we do it from a profound imaged, determined place that is not gray and it's not filled with doubt and it's not tedious. To create our list as spiritual beings is the highest we could ever ask for, because then we know something's going to happen with it. We don't do very well when we try our list on our human self because it tears it apart. Then we go to sleep; the body goes to sleep. We've cast and spun a spell around it that it will be protected, healed, rested, rejuvenated, and filled with vitality when we return. And we've given ourself actual permission to be something else while our body rests.

Because, you see, the Spirit doesn't really rest. On the great Plane when we have done the review in the light, we have to go and rest. It is not about sleeping. We're not going and sleeping for two or three centuries. We are at rest. We are *at-one-ment*. We don't have to do anything. We're giving our body that opportunity, but for us we are gone. We are free to take adventures. We are free to go wherever we want to go. And if we simply acknowledge that we are the holy Spirit, then we are within the natural realm of that activity, and the more we do it, the more we get to play, the more we get to be it.

Now I've given you one full teaching and the measure of at least how do we do this morally, how do we do it justly, how are we honorable, how do we discharge our duties — we still do that as a spiritual person — and given you an understanding, a lot of food for thought.

What I want you to do then is I want you to obviously take a period of contemplation. I want you to take the time to contemplate. Contemplate everything I've taught you because you're going to have to do some drawings on it. Contemplate everything I've said. Take your notes out and review them, think about them, how do they apply to you. There are rich answers here to every one of your problems. No one in here has a problem that is greater than the teaching I taught you today. I have covered the ground well.

Now you contemplate, because in doing so you become utterly spiritual at that point. And don't be afraid, even though your heart starts to beat a little fast, to start taking a look at some of the dark areas in your life, the shadow areas. Start looking at what you really have been doing and look at why you have a past. Don't be afraid to look at it. Let it come out. Because when we clean that closet out, we're at liberty to have Bliss. Do you understand?

W e have now a list here of four things:

- ♦ Free will and choice
- ♦ Defining self
- ♦ Unfinished Business
- ♦ Resolution

I want you to take each of these four things and separately image them.

For example, resolution is going to be a little difficult. I want you to draw pictures of it. I want you to draw a choice to be here. What does that look like to you up here? What does free will and choice look like? Because if you have to think about that, then you're going to have a new definition on its meaning, its performance.

Defining self. Well, how do we draw self? One of the most endearing symbols, of course, is we can use the blue star. But I like the heart, because God is love and the heart also sits by the fourth seal. So what if we start out with the premise that the self is a heart. Let's begin with that concept and then let's tear it apart. Let's fracture it and break it down and move bits and pieces of it over here to demonstrate that a piece of my heart, a piece of my God, is empowering my victimization, or over here my tyranny, or over here my greed, or over here something else. Then it is up to you to meticulously create your past and where your energy's locked up, and don't leave anything out. And take a piece of my heart to show that the only reason that that past is in place is because it has been sanctioned by divine energy.

And if we can show that effectively on a drawing, we get then a great visual, inspired by the master and followed through by the student, on a great profound teaching, that if we can put it into a picture and draw it, it will be one of the greatest mandalas we will ever do because it's ours. It's real and it is about us and our journey.

Then we make another drawing on defining it. Well, defining it is going to encompass these two aspects right here. First we've got to get the energy back, so we start to see in picture after picture what we must do to bring our heart back and to put it where it is now perfect again. And so we have to see measure by measure what we must do to get our energy back. And you must draw those pictures of it.

Those pictures then are going to also include number three, unfinished business, because the unfinished business is the encumbered self. It is the past self; it is the past unfinished. And we're going to have to draw pictures of those. What is unfinished? What have you started that you're in the midst of and can't get out of? Where are you still human and where are you not God? What seems to be in this life your great learnings? Where are your weaknesses? That will point to the unfinished business and the encumbered self. And I want you to draw not a caricature of some fictional entity but a caricature of yourself and what lies unfinished. And however you depict that, it's going to be all right. And then I want you to draw resolution. Perhaps the greatest way to draw resolution is to redraw the heart. Radiant and shining inside of an undersized body there is an oversized heart that talks about a place of spiritual peace. Or perhaps we can draw the body and mimic it as the temple, and that shining through its spires and its windows is the radiant light of spiritual power. Perhaps that's how we see it. Or perhaps we see resolution as the rolling up of some ancient scroll long left undone and seeing it rolling up. Or maybe we see then a cage opening and the flight of a dove.

However we picture it, it must be a picture that is meaningful to us. And when we do it correctly, then we'll understand our own journey. Mandalas should not be made en masse. They are personalized aspects of one's own journey. They should be created by ourselves. Do you understand?

The Gift of the Master

It's important for the master to be a master but not an intimidating one. It is important for the master — whose greatest phenomenon will be the endless show of wisdom, that's the gift of the master — not to intimidate but to encourage. And I tell you, I do so ask that you feel encouraged by what you have learned today and that you feel that you are in a place that's safe enough for you to address this and that you are safe enough to be encouraged to want to change, because I tell you you're never going to disappoint me. Oh, I have left these events and at moments had to go refigure my dream, keep downsizing it. But you're never going to disappoint me because I'm not at a place that I could ever be disappointed. Thank God. And so with that, you see, you have the freedom to be yourself and the freedom to go and change, and my love is not going to change for you. It does not float in and out in the tide. It is not fickle. I love you. I desire that you feel comfortable enough to be inspired by who I am and what I am, even though you can't see me, because that is the kingdom of the Spirit. That's what is radiating out here in front of you that is so beautiful. And that perhaps in this ideal you'll want it enough to be impassioned enough to take a stand and do it. I want to give you the room to do that. Just thought I should tell you that.

So be it.

I love you.

VII.
Epilogue

O my beloved God,
I awaken to your presence
in the present.
O my beloved God,
deliver me from my past
and reclaim my kingdom.
O my beloved God,
bring forward in me
the great virtues
that I shall be *deservant* of.
O my beloved God,
God bless my body
and change my life.
So be it.

To life.

In your contemplation or in that which is termed your drawing of your defining yourself, did you, when you looked back and began the process of releasing, feel lighter or a weight being lifted off of you? So be it. Did you know you've been carrying that weight, and perhaps a lot more, around for a long time? Did you also know that in mystical language we call that veils?

Most entities don't know whatever happened to their happiness. They just know that one day — they don't remember what day — it just disappeared. It is as if childhood had ended somehow. And so they get used to supporting those burdens or supporting those attitudes or indeed those ways of life, and they don't understand really how to get joy. They think that joy lies in other people and they think that joy lies in things. They think that joy lies in recognition. They think that joy lies in success.

And so we begin to understand now how individuals start in pursuit of happiness, how they are in pursuit of aspects of life that can never make them happy. You know, once you get the very thing that you want, it soon loses its glitter. So how do you keep feeding the habit? And it's the same way that entities apply themselves in relationships, apply themselves in eating, apply themselves in habit. It's when do you have enough. Well, you never will have enough because really that isn't the solution.

The solution is that you're gray in the rainbow and you don't even know it. You can see all those other bright colors, but you don't know that you're the one that's gray and it's because we unburden, remove our divinity, and put it in blame, put it in all the aspects that we have addressed so arduously here, and we don't even realize that that was a giving away of a vital life source.

It's the reason why I conceived that the heart was such an appropriate, as it were, term for the God within, the power within, because, you know, we can never give what is not ours.

But the greatest gift that we give is our energy, and when we give it cognizantly we give it in the name of love. Well, we have loved our enslavements and our burdens into life, haven't we? So this lightness that you're feeling, I want to tell you, my beloved masters, can you not use that then as a talisman, say to yourself,

"Why am I feeling heavy today? Why am I feeling heavy?" It has nothing to do with indigestion. Or "Why am I feeling heavy today?" Well, just reflect backwards, see where you became fractured. That will show you where it is. And it can be as simple as being dishonest. That will fracture the energy and will cause the veil or the load to return. Now aren't you happy that you know that?

Now again most people are under this reality and it's served them for so long they're really afraid of what they would be like without it. Because, you know, what if suddenly in a struggling relationship — whether that relationship be a business relationship, a family relationship, a lovers' relationship, a neighborly relationship, or a communal relationship — what if suddenly the dynamics of having the relationship is that it was based on argumentative opinions, and then suddenly you wake up one morning and you unload yourself and you burst into absolute joy? What are you going to do to that relationship?

Do you understand the subtleties of what I'm talking about here? Because it's almost as if they expect you to grind or expect you to be coarse or expect you to have this sort of argumentative defensive attitude. And when suddenly you're not that any longer, there is an aspect of us that the brain always works, is always manipulating, to see how it's going to fit into the larger plan.

So for those of you who do not unveil yourself because it's serving you, it's your choice. Now you have the knowledge. You can never say I never knew better because now you do. Do you understand that?

So be it.

The Magic Presence

I tell you that the more and the more that you do this, the lighter and lighter and lighter you're going to become. And that lightness allows your rib cage to expand broadly and that deep draft of air to be taken in, which means that a great deal of energy is coming home. And that lightness of being brings about what we call the magical presence — the magical presence.

So we talked then yesterday, using a familiar diagram, that

this was the past that you keep returning to and that the heart is fractured in this place here.

The divine energy is fractured here because it's supporting time. Time cannot be supported unless it has consciousness. So all of our energy is back here. Well, we're learning to fracture it and replace it here. Got the picture so far? Now the energy keeps coming home; this starts to radiate. When it does, we become multidimensional. So all of the gifts that we set up for ourself begin to fall in the magic presence.

Now this is really important. In the godhead there is no time. Time then becomes actionable by energy and consciousness split. When we dissolve yesterday and we find ourselves in a splendid moment, right here, all of our potentials are going to fall into that present because, you see, they were created in a presence that is identical to them on the higher Planes of Bliss. Do you understand?

Now this magic presence is the magic presence that is attainable by focusing into the Void and abolishing that which is termed the past identity. That means focusing without people, places, things, times, and events. People, places, things, times, and events absolutely erase a quiet and silent place in you. If we can hold this magic presence, it is in this place all of the great and wonderful unimaginables take place.

Reason this for yourself. The unimaginable cannot take place in a time belt called the past. Furthermore, it can't take place if there's no homecoming for it. It only takes place when there is room. And that room the ancients understand as that which is termed the place of nonbeing. And we say nonbeing because we identify being with people, places, things, times, and events. Do you understand? This is the magic presence.

This is the magic presence that you are able to achieve in analogical mind.[12] You get out of the magic presence when you are astounded that you were able to do it. Then you got wrapped up in being astounded. Do you understand that? This is the magical presence that absolute and complete

---

[12] Analogical mind is a state of being in which the student becomes one with her/his desired manifestation.

restoration happens. It is in this magical presence that all time is now. Do you understand?

If your past comes back into your face two days later, what are you going to do? If you start feeling the attitude, what are you going to do? You can go to the Void, focus on the Void without people, places, things, times, and events and the magical moment will appear. It dissolves all of its energies. Or put it there and then focus on the attitude without anybody, without it being anyplace, without it having to do with anything or any event and see if it can hold up. It won't be able to hold up. You have a tool now. If you don't use it, then you have elected to lead your own path. It's all right.

And what I wanted to say to you is that no matter what you do, it will always be all right. I wanted you to know that. And that this teaching was not about blaming you; it was about helping you, giving you great wisdom. You never want to walk away when it's being delivered because you can always learn from it — you are not that wise yet — to be able to help you out of your distresses and help you into your list, that your list manifests straightaway and that all the things on the Plane of Bliss you get because you deserve them.

But you only deserve them if you understand the mechanics, as it were, that you're standing in your own way and that you're the one that's really responsible for the heartbreak that you feel and indeed that you're the one that's responsible for feeling so powerless. There's no one, no entity, that is there holding the purse strings on your life. There's no entity holding back the purposeful good in your life. No one is doing that. No one has the capacity to do that. And the only one who has that is you because it is, after all, your reality.

And so it is you who build the dams for the sake of argument. And it is you who build the dams for the sake of not wanting to be wrong. It is you who build the dams to cover up your failure. It is you who build the dams so that you never have to look at yourself. And that's the only entity that does it.

The whole of the universe is not going to stop because of you. And the whole of great life is going to go on in spite of you, no matter what you do. No matter how stalwart you are in your stubbornness, we are going to go on, and you get to be left in the saffron dust because, after all, no matter what you do, you can only do to you. Got the picture?

That's why it takes a very humble person to become great, humble and wise to know that arguing for the sake of arguing for limitations is not wise and that it is just as soon that you take a look than trying to defend yourself and say it's not there.

This teaching was about giving you the tools and the knowledge to understand and explain many things to you so that many mysteries no longer are vague to you. Oh, it's for certain that I could have done a much more splendid job on explaining Bliss, but I don't really need to. It's enough for you to know that it exists and what a place that could be. That is the unimaginable imaginable, and that's for you to experience. It's enough to know that you were once there and many times and that there is a direction to your life.

And when you get into a place of clarity, it will come in the form called knowingness. You'll just know. You won't have to say, "Well, I know because I have a hunch," or "Indeed I know because I feel it. I just know." That should suffice because if you go back in the past to try and figure out how you know, you're not going to find the knowingness backwards. Do you understand that?

Well, all of this is set up for you and much, much more. I tell you, my beloved people, you haven't seen anything that you can do. You haven't even begun to imagine your wonderful life. I know that your body feels bad. And I know that you're weary and I know that you're struggling, you know, trying to put it all together. But you're really getting in your own way. It's a very simple process and that when applied with utter simplicity, you have all of the answers. And it's not hard to do at all. You can become God in a moment. All you have to do is to declare passionately, "This is what I am," and then to have the courage to *impassionately* be it every day and every moment. It's the continuity of it.

You don't even know how outrageous your lives are going to become. Furthermore, you don't know what you're missing that's been going on behind your back a long time, because you're so zeroed in and focused on these little, little, tiny issues. And you make them so large, you know, they block the whole view. But, you know, you can do extraordinary things. Your wildest dreams will all come true and then you're going to have to dream more wild dreams. But it's all possible, and all you need to do is give yourself a chance to taste that honey. It is a new wine.

And you too will come to a profound wisdom and you won't be as reactive as you were in the past to infantile situations. You will have matured and you can see it and understand it and thereby not be a part of it. You'll outgrow it because you're going to outgrow your past. When you do that, you'll start to mature. Do you understand that?

And illness of body and all of those things, they too will pass, for I have explained to you how regeneration occurs and why it occurs. They too will pass. And so many things will become even in your life or, for a term, what you would say, balance. They will indeed. You must understand the path of the master is not a hard one; it's getting started that's so hard. It's like those internal combustion machines that you pull that rope on. I watch some of you doing that. "What are they doing?" You know, you keep pulling it and pulling it and pulling it and it just putt-putts and then dies on you. I've known horses like that. It's that sort of same analogy.

The hardest part is getting started. Because when you arrive at the magical presence and it starts to get magical — and if you're keenly aware you'll just keep being that — and then it's just going to fall from heaven. It's just everything, all the great and bountiful things your God set up for you. And it isn't hard.

The path of the master is to conquer oneself and to always guard against the encroachment of a neuronet — to which they raised themself up in a lifetime with — and to always be on guard like the great soldiers that they are, that they conquer it and they never let it get out of hand. They never let that attitude start to fracture them. And, see, it's not about anyone in their life; it's about them in their life. You see? Everyone else will just push buttons, but they're really innocent. It's the master who doesn't want that button to ever be pushed again.

And they know exactly what to do. And the more they do it, that little thing gets to going. Why it can run a long time. Just sit there and crank. They do the same thing. And if they run out of fuel, they'll go into a rest period. That means they go into silence. They'll go into nature or they'll go into a quiet, quiet, place and they bring it all up and they address it and they know how to address it. And they will not rest until they have eked out of the shadows every last remnant because they know they are losing their power because of it. And they have great things on their agenda they desire to achieve or they know that in order to have the great things that are awaiting them, they've got to be fully capable of executing them as experience. Do you understand?

So they retire and regroup. "I am that which I am. I am not defined by people, places, things, times, and events. I am that which I am." And they know when it's finished because the veil is lifted because the energy comes back home and they are recharged and they are ready to emerge from that profound silence, meditation, and discipline, and then they reemerge back out. That's what they do.

And the hardest people to deal with are their families. But you should know that in some parts of the world, to have raised a child to masterhood is the greatest achievement of that family's line, contrary to the West, who finds it humiliating, disturbing, and *nonconformitive*. It's going to be the most difficult thing to do.

But don't you know that when you really honor your parents, you honor them. Be grateful to them for their passion, for their ability, your mother to carry you in her womb and your father to help deliver you and feed you and clothe you and shelter you. They're worth the honoring. Anything they do after that is all forgivable because after that they're really Gods as well, and we honor them. We see the highest good in them and that, of course, then is the highest love.

And our brothers and sisters, they all found a place to come into. And, as you know, they too more than likely were in those woods of contemplation endeavoring to figure something out, and they deserve the right to have their opinion.

If you are utterly self-empowered, what any man says about you will never move you from your center and it won't fracture you. And then that is just a state of radiating love. And when you can still love them and bless them for their opinion, then you are a true kindred of the highest order. But you should not move down to their level for the sake of kindredship. You have to bloom in their midst, in spite of them and for them. And I promise you that one sweet hour they'll call upon you and you will have the power in that need to do marvelous things. And therein lies the gift of being your own master.

I expect for you to apply diligently what you have learned here because it is given from a greater and more priceless place than this place that we know. Use it. If you don't, you have nothing to complain about when your life, instead of getting greater as a result of the teachings, seems to become diminished by them.

So be it.

Other Ramtha Titles

The following is a list of additional books on Ramtha available through Ramtha's School of Enlightenment and other fine bookstores. Also available is a whole library of recordings and videos of Ramtha's teachings. All products are available through mail order at:

Ramtha's School of Enlightenment
PO Box 519
Yelm, Washington 98597
(800) 347-0439 or (360) 458-4771
email: greg@ramtha.com
Website: http://www.ramtha.com

RAMTHA *Edited by Stephen Lee Weinberg (217 pages).* The classic work on Ramtha, that Ramtha himself has referred to as "The Great White Book." A brilliant work designed to inform the general public as to the nature of Ramtha's teachings along with a rich sampling of his wisdom on many topics. Highly recommended for those ready to understand this great teacher and his message. It is one of the most important books to read if you are preparing to enter the school.

#1401 - Hardcover	$ 19.95
#1401 - Softcover	$ 12.50
#1401 - Leather-Bound Edition	$ 29.95

RAMTHA: AN INTRODUCTION *Edited by Stephen Lee Weinberg (228 pages).* An engaging collection of teachings that will appeal equally to those familiar or unfamiliar with Ramtha. More than an introduction; a true treasure of personal mastery.

#1404 - Softcover	$ 9.95

I AM RAMTHA *Edited by Richard Cohn, Cindy Black, and Greg Simmons. (127 pages).* This book is a beautifully photographed book that accompanies thirteen of Ramtha's most universal teachings. Wonderful teachings on the subject of feelings, being at one with nature, unconditional love, and the prize that is called life.

#1201 - Hardcover	$ 9.95

THE ANCIENT SCHOOLS OF WISDOM *Compiled by Diane Munoz (172 pages)* is a teaching and introduction to the formation of Ramtha's School of Enlightenment. Ramtha tells the history of how the ancient schools operated in times past and why their instruction was so precious: to awaken the forgotten God within.
#7100 - Softcover $ 9.95

A STATE OF MIND *JZ Knight (445 pages)*. The intimate account of JZ's life in her own words. Her story, which includes her humorous and poignant introduction to Ramtha, is a story of the triumph of the human Spirit. Also available in an edited audio version, recorded in her own voice.
#1501 - Hardcover $ 9.95
#1501.1 - Cassette (120 minutes) $ 9.95

TO LIFE *Compiled by Diane Munoz.* At the beginning of each audience, Ramtha elegantly and thought-provokingly salutes the God within with a toast. This book is a selection of the toasts from Ramtha's audiences from May 1988 through May 1996. A wonderful way to start your day!
#7101 - Softcover $15.95

CHANGE: THE DAYS TO COME *Ramtha (149 pages)*. Based on the 3-day intensive taught in Denver, May 1986. This book tells of man's destruction of Earth's resources and nature's recourse to heal herself. This book has never been more timely than now.
#1402 - Softcover $10.00

LAST WALTZ OF THE TYRANTS *Edited by Judy Pope Koteen (153 pages)*. This book is a synthesis of Ramtha's teachings on the challenges we face by those who control the world economy and from the coming radical changes in nature. It provides inspiration and practical guidelines to enable you to be prepared.
#1202 - Softcover

                                                                           $ 7.95
MANIFESTING: A MASTER'S MANUAL *Edited by Khit Harding (100 pages)*. Based on the November 1986 intensive, The Power To Manifest, this is compiled such that each page serves as a thought-provoking concept for contemplation and understanding.
#1102 - Softcover $ 9.95

SOULMATES: THE INTENSIVE *Ramtha (128 pages).*
Based on the 3-day intensive taught by Ramtha in Seattle, WA, January 1986, this book spells out the mystery of the science of soulmates and its importance in knowing and loving self.
#1403 - Softcover $10.00

SPINNER OF TALES *Compiled by Deborah Kerins (228 pages).*
Ramtha has captivated audiences throughout the years with his telling of tales. Now they have been put together in book form to be preserved and delight readers of all ages. These stories are from the earliest years of the teachings to the most recent. A true treasure!
#1300 - Softcover $10.00

UFO'S AND THE NATURE OF REALITY *Edited by Judy Pope Koteen (221 pages).* This book is a sometimes shocking, sometimes comforting picture of what we would call alien intervention in our history, in our present, and in our future. It allows us to see what is "out there." But this is more than another UFO book. It exposes the limitations of subjective mind and encourages the reader to move into interdimensional mind, the source from which all is available. This book will alter the way you've perceived everything you've been told.
#1611 - Softcover $11.00

Foreign Language Products

We have a large selection of Ramtha books in German and Spanish, a smaller selection in Italian, French, and Japanese. We also carry audio cassettes and videos in German and Spanish.

If you are interested in knowing more about Ramtha's School of Enlightenment, for a free introductory brochure and a cassette tape on The Ancient Schools of Wisdom, call or write to:

Ramtha's School of Enlightenment
PO Box 1210
Yelm, WA 98597
(360) 458-5201, ext.10
email: michele@ramtha.com